Mr. Lincoln and His War

Mr. Lincoln and His War

John Chandler Griffin

PELICAN PUBLISHING COMPANY
GRETNA 2009

I humbly dedicate this little volume to the five wonderful women in my life: Betty, Alexis, Kori Rochel, Emmalee Grace, and Serrah Roxanne.

*The word "Pelican" and the depiction of a pelican
are trademarks of Pelican Publishing Company, Inc.,
and are registered in the U.S. Patent and Trademark Office.*

Library of Congress Cataloging-in-Publication Data

Griffin, John Chandler, 1936-
  Mr. Lincoln and his war / John Chandler Griffin.
      p. cm.
  Includes bibliographical references.
  ISBN 978-1-58980-711-2 (hardcover : alk. paper) 1. Lincoln, Abraham, 1809-1865. 2. Lincoln, Abraham, 1809-1865—Pictorial works. 3. Presidents—United States—Biography. I. Title.
  E457.G843 2009
  973.7092—dc22
  [B]

                              2009024062

Frontispiece: Abraham Lincoln, 1863 (Library of Congress)

Printed in the United States of America
Published by Pelican Publishing Company, Inc.
1000 Burmaster Street, Gretna, Louisiana 70053

Any people, anywhere, being inclined and having the power, have the right to rise up and shake off the existing government and form a new one that suits them better. This is a most valuable, a most sacred right—a right which we hope and believe is to liberate the world. Nor is this right confined to cases in which the whole people of an existing government may choose to exercise it. Any portion of such people, that can, may revolutionize, and make their own of so much of the territory as they inhabit.

Abraham Lincoln
in a speech to Congress in 1848

Contents

Timeline

1809   Abraham Lincoln is born to Thomas Lincoln and Nancy Hanks on February 12 in a log cabin on the Nolin River in Hardin County, Kentucky.

1810   The total population of the United States is 7,239,822 people, of whom 1,191,363 are black slaves.

1811   Thomas Lincoln moves his family to a place on Knob Creek near Hogenville, Kentucky. • In November the great Battle of Tippecanoe is waged.

1812   Lincoln's younger brother, Thomas, dies in infancy. • Congress declares war against England, and the New England states threaten to secede from the union.

1813   Andrew Jackson's Tennessee militia moves against the Creek Indians, military action that will end with 1814's Battle of Horseshoe Bend. • Fort Niagara is captured by the British.

1814   Lincoln briefly attends school. • The British burn the White House, and Francis Scott Key composes "The Star-Spangled Banner." On Christmas Eve a peace treaty is signed between England and the United States, officially ending the War of 1812.

1815   Before news of the peace reaches America, Andrew Jackson defeats the British at New Orleans. • The United States declares war against Algiers to protect American merchants from Barbary pirates.

1816   The Lincolns move from Kentucky to Indiana, near Little Pigeon Creek. • Indiana is admitted to the union.

1817   War breaks out between U.S. forces and the Seminole Indians in Florida. • Henry Clay organizes the American Colonization Society in Washington. Its purpose is to send freed slaves to Africa.

1818   On October 5, Lincoln's mother dies of milk sickness. • Mary Todd is born in Lexington, Kentucky, on December 13.

Thomas Lincoln marries Sarah Bush Johnson. She brings with her three children: Elizabeth, John, and Matilda. • Alabama is admitted to the union as the twenty-second state.   **1819**

Eleven-year-old Lincoln daily walks many miles through the forest to school. He will soon read *The Pilgrim's Progress, Aesop's Fables, Arabian Nights,* and *Robinson Crusoe.* • The number of slaves in the United States is 2,900,031.   **1820**

Missouri is admitted to the union as the twenty-fourth state, entering as a Slave State. Antislavery agitation in that state becomes violent.   **1821**

Thomas Lincoln rents his son out to work on neighboring farms. • Abraham Lincoln begins attending a school run by James Swansy and spends much of his spare time reading books.   **1822**

Lincoln attends Andrew Crawford's neighborhood school. • The Monroe Doctrine is enunciated.   **1823**

The Protective Tariff Bill is adopted, though opposed by both the Southern and New England states.   **1824**

Abraham Lincoln turns sixteen. • John Quincy Adams is inaugurated as the nation's sixth president.   **1825**

Lincoln begins studying his first law book. • Lincoln's sister, Sarah, marries neighbor Aaron Grigsby on August 2. • Thomas Jefferson and John Adams die on the same day.   **1826**

For nine months, Lincoln works for James Taylor as a farmhand at the mouth of Anderson Creek. He earns his first dollar ferrying passengers to a steamer on the Ohio River.   **1827**

On January 28, Lincoln's sister, Sarah, dies in childbirth. • Lincoln, along with Allen and James Gentry, makes the trip to New Orleans carrying cargo aboard a flatboat. They are attacked by seven blacks along the way, but the aggressors are driven back. In New Orleans, Lincoln witnesses his first slave auction.   **1828**

William Lloyd Garrison advocates the immediate emancipation of all slaves. Mexico issues the first proclamation of emancipation on the North American continent.   **1829**

The Lincolns move to the Sangamon River in Illinois. Abraham, now a man of twenty-one, works in the forest felling trees and splitting rails. The family soon moves to Goose Nest Prairie in Coles County.   **1830**

Lincoln helps his father build a cabin in the Illinois wilderness.   **1831**

For himself, he builds a flatboat for use on the Sangamon River. In the spring he loads the boat with pork, corn, and live hogs, which he takes to New Salem for sale. He settles in New Salem and boards at Rutledge's Tavern, where he becomes acquainted with Ann Rutledge. He votes for the first time.

1832 Lincoln joins the Illinois militia for the Black Hawk War. He is elected captain but sees no military action during three months of service. He will be paid $125 for his time in the militia. • On August 6 he becomes a candidate for the Illinois House of Representatives but is defeated. • Lincoln and William F. Berry buy an interest in a New Salem store, but the men go broke.

1833 Burdened with debt, Lincoln learns and practices surveying. • On May 7, Lincoln is appointed postmaster in New Salem.

1834 Lincoln is elected to the Illinois House of Representatives and becomes known as one of the "Long Nine," a group of politicians from the Springfield area who are over six feet tall. He leaves for the state capital, then at Vandalia.

1835 On August 25, Ann Rutledge dies and Lincoln, according to one biographer, is heartbroken and melancholy.

1836 On September 9, Lincoln receives his license to practice law and is reelected to the state legislature. • Gen. Sam Houston defeats Santa Anna at the Battle of San Jacinto and then becomes the first president of the Republic of Texas.

1837 On April 15, Lincoln moves to Springfield and becomes the law partner of John Todd Stuart. He begins rooming with Josh Speed. • Martin Van Buren is inaugurated as the eighth president of the United States. • To his great relief, Mary Owens rejects Lincoln's marriage proposal.

1838 Elected to his third term, Lincoln becomes the leading Whig in the state legislature. He continues to practice law in Springfield.

1839 Abolitionists organize the Liberty Party in New York • Lincoln qualifies to practice law in the circuit court of the United States. • Lincoln meets Mary Todd of Lexington, Kentucky, for the first time.

1840 Lincoln is elected to his fourth term in the Illinois House of Representatives. • He becomes engaged to Mary Todd.

1841 Lincoln dissolves his partnership with John T. Stuart and becomes partners with Stephen T. Logan. • In the state legislature, Lincoln meets his future political rival Stephen A. Douglas. • William Henry Harrison is inaugurated as the country's ninth president but dies a month later. He is succeeded by John Tyler.

On November 4, Lincoln marries Mary Todd, and they move into the Globe Tavern for four dollars per week. • Lincoln addresses the Temperance Society of Springfield, favoring total abstinence. **1842**

Lincoln's first son, Robert Todd Lincoln, is born at the Globe Tavern on August 1. • Lincoln dissolves his law partnership with Logan. **1843**

Lincoln purchases his Springfield home from the Reverend Dresser for fifteen hundred dollars. • In December he becomes the law partner of William Herndon, who will become his first biographer. **1844**

James K. Polk becomes the eleventh president. • Florida, with slavery permitted, becomes the twenty-seventh state. **1845**

The Lincolns have their first photographs taken. • Lincoln's second son, Edward Baker Lincoln, is born on March 10. • On August 3, Lincoln is elected to the U.S. House of Representatives as the only Whig among seven Democrats representing Illinois. • War breaks out between the United States and Mexico. Gen. Zachary Taylor's army moves into Mexico and captures Monterey. **1846**

Lincoln goes to Washington as a congressman. He loudly denounces the Mexican War and President Polk. • Gen. Winfield Scott captures Mexico City. • The first Mormons arrive at Salt Lake. **1847**

Lincoln campaigns for the Whig presidential candidate, Zachary Taylor. He also introduces a bill for the abolition of slavery in the District of Columbia. • Gold is discovered in California. • A peace treaty is signed with Mexico. • Karl Marx writes the *Communist Manifesto.* • That summer the Lincolns and their two sons visit New York. **1848**

Lincoln is defeated in his bid to become commissioner of the General Land Office and returns to Springfield. On March 7 he is admitted to practice law before the U.S. Supreme Court. • Zachary Taylor becomes the twelfth president. • Lincoln receives a patent for a device to buoy boats over shallow water. **1849**

On February 1, Lincoln's second son, Edward Baker, dies at the age of four. • On December 1, his third son, William Wallace ("Willie"), is born. • Millard Fillmore becomes the thirteenth president of the United States. • California becomes the thirty-first state. • Congress passes the Fugitive Slave Law. In 1850 there are 3,204,333 slaves in the United States. **1850**

Lincoln is busy as a circuit lawyer. • On January 17 his father dies at the age of seventy-three of a kidney ailment. Lincoln does not attend the funeral. **1851**

1852   Lincoln joins the Sons of Temperance in Springfield. • *Uncle Tom's Cabin* becomes a bestseller and influences citizens against slavery. • Henry Clay dies at the age of seventy-five and Daniel Webster at seventy.

1853   Lincoln's fourth son, Thomas ("Tad"), is born on April 4. • Franklin Pierce becomes the fourteenth president. • The Gadsden Purchase secures additional territories from Mexico for the United States.

1854   Lincoln is elected to the Illinois legislature but declines the office on November 27 in order to run for the U.S. Senate. • The Missouri Compromise is repealed and Lincoln's interest in politics is aroused by the passage of the Kansas-Nebraska Act. He is instrumental in forming the Republican Party as a party against slavery.

1855   Lincoln gives more than fifty speeches in support of the Republican nominee for president, John C. Frémont. • Lyman Trumbull defeats Lincoln in his run for the U.S. Senate.

1856   The first Republican National Convention is held in Philadelphia. • The Territory of Kansas is declared to be in a state of insurrection.

1857   The *Dred Scott* decision confirms abolitionist feeling in the North. Lincoln becomes an outspoken opponent of the ruling. • James Buchanan becomes the fifteenth president of the United States.

1858   Lincoln is successful in the Armstrong murder trial. • Nominated as a Republican for the U.S. Senate, Lincoln challenges his Democratic opponent Stephen Douglas to seven debates. These debates make Lincoln's name known and respected throughout the country. He is defeated in the election, though he receives the popular majority.

1859   John Brown is hanged for his raid at Harpers Ferry. • Oregon becomes the thirty-third state. • Jefferson Davis addresses the Democratic State Convention of Mississippi on behalf of slavery and the extension of the slave territory.

1860   On February 27, Lincoln delivers his Cooper Union speech in New York. • On May 22 the Republican Party nominates him for president in Chicago. He is elected president on November 5, receiving 40 percent of the popular vote. • South Carolina secedes from the union on December 20. Representatives from seven Southern states urge the formation of a southern Confederacy. • On December 26, Maj. Robert Anderson of the U.S. Army occupies Fort Sumter.

The *Star of the West*, the supply ship bound for Fort Sumter, is fired upon by Southern artillery. • Lincoln visits his stepmother, Sarah Bush Johnston Lincoln. On February 11 he departs Springfield for Washington. • On February 18, Jefferson Davis is inaugurated as president of the Confederate States of America. • Lincoln is inaugurated as the sixteenth president of the United States on March 4. • There are thirty-three states in the union, eighteen free and fifteen slave, before South Carolina and six other Southern states secede. • In April, Maj. Robert Anderson surrenders Fort Sumter. Lincoln orders a blockade of Virginia and North Carolina and calls for seventy-five thousand volunteers. He violates the Constitution when he declares martial law and suspends the writ of habeas corpus. He again violates the Constitution when he orders Federal troops across state lines into Bull Run, Virginia. There the Confederates win a great victory. • George McClellan is appointed commander in chief of Union forces.

1861

On January 13, Edwin Stanton becomes secretary of war. • In February, Lincoln's son Willie dies at the White House of typhoid fever. • McClellan begins his Peninsula Campaign. • In April, New Orleans is captured by Gen. Benjamin "Beast" Butler. • Slavery is abolished in the District of Columbia. • In June, Gen. Robert E. Lee becomes commander of the Confederate armies. • In August the Union army is again beat at Bull Run. • A September loss at Antietam forces Lee's army to turn back from its first Northern invasion. • Gen. Ambrose Burnside replaces General McClelland as commander of Union forces. • In December, General Lee's army wins at Fredericksburg. • Confederates under Gen. Braxton Bragg retreat at Murfreesboro. • Lincoln proposes to compensate Slave States for the emancipation of their slaves.

1862

On January 1, Lincoln's Emancipation Proclamation goes into effect. • Gen. Joseph Hooker replaces Burnside as head of the Army of the Potomac. • On March 3 the Draft Act is enacted, calling every healthy male in the North to military service. It will be met with riots in New York and elsewhere. • In May, General Lee defeats General Hooker at Chancellorsville. Gen. Stonewall Jackson is killed in that battle, a terrible blow to the Confederacy. • In July, Meade defeats Lee at Gettysburg. Grant and Sherman capture Vicksburg. • The Federals are defeated at Chickamauga in September. • That October, Lincoln calls for another three hundred thousand men. • In November, Lincoln delivers his Gettysburg Address.

1863

Fort Fisher in North Carolina falls to Union forces in January. • In February, Lincoln calls for another five hundred thousand volunteers. Over the past four months Lincoln has increased his number of soldiers by almost a million men, while the South has no reserves to call on. • In March, Gen. Ulysses Grant is

1864

named commander in chief of the Union army. • In April, Gen. Philip Sheridan is named commander of cavalry in the Army of the Potomac. • In May, the Union army suffers terrible losses at the Battle of the Wilderness. • The siege of Petersburg begins in June. • Lincoln receives the Republican nomination to run for a second term as president. • Delaware is placed under martial law. • In August, Sheridan takes command of the Shenandoah Campaign. • Gen. John B. Hood replaces Gen. Joe Johnston in the defense of Atlanta. In September, General Sherman captures and burns the city. • In November, Federal forces capture Nashville. • Lincoln easily defeats George B. McClellan in the presidential election.

1865   In January, Francis P. Blair submits his report to Lincoln on peace negotiations with Jefferson Davis, which leads to the Hampton Roads Conference in February. Lincoln attends. • Lincoln is inaugurated on March 4. • The Thirteenth Amendment, prohibiting slavery, is adopted by Congress but is not ratified until December. • In March, Lincoln delivers his Second Inaugural Address. • Lincoln pardons all army deserters who will return to the ranks within sixty days. • In April, Richmond falls to Union forces. • On April 9, General Lee surrenders his Army of Northern Virginia at Appomattox Court House. • Lincoln is shot at Ford's Theatre on April 14 and dies the next morning. On April 21 a nine-car funeral train leaves Washington and begins a seventeen-hundred-mile journey to Springfield. • Andrew Johnson is inaugurated as the seventeenth president on April 15. • On April 26, John Wilkes Booth is shot and killed in Garrett's tobacco barn near Bowling Green, Virginia. • On May 4, Lincoln is buried at Oak Ridge near his home in Springfield. • In June, Galveston, Texas, the last post held by the Confederates, surrenders. (Gen. Stand Watie and his Confederate Cherokees in Oklahoma refuse to surrender until July, thereby becoming the last Confederate unit to surrender.) • Four of the Lincoln conspirators are hanged and four are sentenced to life in prison.

Abraham Lincoln, a Brief Portrait

Whether the reader loves or despises Abraham Lincoln makes little difference. The objective reader will certainly agree that he was truly one of the most unique human beings ever to draw breath on this earth. He was born dirt poor to an illiterate farmer, Thomas Lincoln, and an illegitimate mother, Nancy Hanks, in a crude, one-room, backwoods cabin on February 12, 1809. Incredibly, fifty-one years later, thanks to his own intellect, ingenuity, wit, and hard work, Lincoln was paid the highest tribute in the land when he was elected president of the United States. Without doubt, his is one of the most inspirational stories ever told, and he has rightfully become a bigger-than-life figure of legend.

Along with his storied status in the nation's history naturally swirl legends, tales, and rumors. His mother, Nancy Hanks, was the illegitimate daughter of a woman who had once been indicted for immoral behavior. Her beginnings could hardly have been more humble, and there were several other illegitimate children in her family, common amongst the backwoods people of the time.

It has been widely rumored for the past two hundred years that Lincoln himself was illegitimate. People who were close to the family swore that Thomas Lincoln had suffered from a severe case of mumps early in life and, as a result, was unable to father children. As proof, these same people pointed out that there was no resemblance whatsoever between Thomas and Abraham. From a physical standpoint, Thomas was a stocky, muscular individual who stood five-nine and weighed about 190 pounds. Abraham stood six-four and was of slim build. And there were differences in their personality and intellect. Thomas was known to be slow both mentally and physically, while Abraham was an industrious young man and extremely inquisitive even as a small child. Judging from the complexity of his ideas and the sophistication of his language, as seen in his writings, his IQ must have been close to genius levels.

There are at least two long-running rumors concerning his paternity. One has it that Lincoln was the son of John C. Calhoun, the brilliant young politician from Abbeville, South Carolina. He had a sexual affair with a young barmaid of his acquaintance, Nancy Hanks, who was employed at a roadhouse where Calhoun frequently spent the night. Hoping to avoid a

scandal when Nancy became pregnant, Calhoun paid a cattle
driver from Kentucky, Thomas Lincoln, several hundred dollars
to take Nancy with him when he returned to his home state.
Thomas did so, and in time he married her.

Another story has it that Nancy Hanks was a young servant
girl in the home of Abraham Enloe of Ocona Lufka, North
Carolina. Thanks to Enloe, she became pregnant. She gave birth
to a male child and, for obvious reasons, named him Abraham.
Even as an infant, this child looked exactly like his father. Enloe's
wife recognized the child's parentage and became furious. She
accused her husband of having an affair with the servant girl
and insisted that he send her away—or face the consequences.
Luckily for Enloe a Kentucky cattle driver in his employ had
just stopped by for a few days. His name was Thomas Lincoln.
Enloe paid him several hundred dollars to leave immediately for
Kentucky and take Nancy Hanks and her baby with him. Lincoln
agreed, and eventually he married the woman.

There is just enough documentation—local history supported
by local historians—to keep both these rumors afloat.

Another rumor that surfaces from time to time concerns
Lincoln's sexuality. He married Mary Todd in 1842 when he was
thirty-three years old, and she was, as far as can be determined,
the first female in whom he had shown any interest, and his
interest in her was strictly financial and political. It must be
remembered that Lincoln as a young man was unusually homely
in appearance, and perhaps it was a fear of rejection that led
to his apparent aversion to females. There had been some talk
of Lincoln and Ann Rutledge in 1835 and some have tried to
create a romantic affair between those two (Carl Sandburg in
particular), but there is nothing to indicate that they were ever
anything more than friends. A few years later, Lincoln in a hasty
moment agreed to marry Mary Owens, a short, obese woman
who had not a tooth in her head. However, Lincoln denied that
there was ever anything of a romantic nature between them.

As for Mary Todd, Lincoln left her waiting at the altar on two
occasions before he finally forced himself to marry her. He knew that
if he married Mary Todd, he would gain the financial and political
support of two of the most influential families in the West, the
Todds of Kentucky and the Edwardses of Illinois. Still, apparently
he was unsure whether or not attaining a high political office was
quite worth being married to a woman such as Mary Todd.

At the time of his engagement to Mary, Lincoln was rooming
with his friend, Josh Speed, an arrangement that lasted for
several years and involved sharing the same bed. As for Josh
Speed, he became engaged to the beautiful Fanny Henning at the
same time Lincoln was courting Mary Todd. But once Lincoln
jilted Mary, Josh Speed did the same to Fanny. In fact, he left
town altogether and returned to his mother's home in Kentucky.

Carl Sandburg's comments concerning the Lincoln-Speed
affair leave the reader puzzled. Sandburg, who always tried

to put the best face on things where Lincoln was concerned, says this concerning Lincoln's relationship with Josh Speed: "A streak of lavender ran through him; he had spots as soft as May violets." He repeated the phrase in description of Speed.

Lincoln also suffered from chronic nightmares. One young lawyer who traveled the circuit with him reported that one night when they were sharing a room, "he awoke to see his companion sitting up in bed, his figure dimly visible by the ghostly firelight, talking the wildest and most incoherent nonsense all to himself. Awakening suddenly, Lincoln jumped out of bed, put some wood on the fire, then sat in front of it, moodily, dejectedly, in a most sombre and gloomy spell, till the breakfast bell rang."

Indeed, he and Mary both had dreams and nightmares, and both, like many country folks, believed that those dreams and nightmares could somehow foretell the future, if only they were wise enough to interpret them. In fact, on the eve of his assassination Lincoln told his wife and secretaries that he had dreamed the previous night that he had entered a dark room, and there he saw himself stretched out in a coffin, dead.

Too, Lincoln and Mary believed in spirits. Following their son Willie's death in 1862, both parents were obviously brokenhearted. Lincoln walked the halls for days weeping for his lost son, and Mary took to bed for weeks. Eventually she hired a medium to come to the White House on eight different occasions to conduct séances. Lincoln himself attended at least one of those. Asked by his secretaries if the medium had contacted Willie, he simply shrugged and said he did not know.

Still, playing a leadership role came quite early and quite naturally to Lincoln, who disliked being called "Abraham" and absolutely despised "Abe." He preferred simply "Lincoln." By the time he was sixteen he already stood six-two, and because of his constant use of the ax, he was extremely strong through the arms, chest, and shoulders. On several occasions he was challenged to fight "the strongest boy in the county" and this he did, winning with no trouble each time.

Because of his great height, the other boys came up only to his chest. But he was never a bully. To the contrary, he was of a cordial disposition, had a great sense of humor and a quick wit, and was everybody's favorite storyteller. It is said that wherever he went, other boys (and many men) would stop work and come to sit near him to listen to his latest jokes and stories. By the time Lincoln was eighteen, it had become a mark of distinction for a boy to say that he was one of Lincoln's best friends.

As Lincoln rose from a penniless, illiterate young carpenter and farmer to one of Illinois' most prominent attorneys and politicians, it became evident that he was a man with a brilliant mind who could match wits and vocabularies with the nation's most well-educated gentlemen.

In 1847, at the age of thirty-eight, he was elected to Congress as a Whig. There he violently opposed the Mexican War, calling it nothing more than a wicked "land grab" on the part of the U.S. government. Like most Whigs he feared that the government might annex Mexico and other Mexican territories and open them up as slave states. Still, he favored Texas's right to secede from Mexico, a position that would come back to haunt him in 1861.

In 1851, while Lincoln was practicing law in Springfield, his stepmother notified him that his father was dying. Lincoln wrote a rather cool letter in return, explaining that because of his busy schedule it would be impossible for him to visit at that time. He did not attend his father's funeral. He loved his stepmother dearly, but his relationship with his father was somewhat complex and contradictory. He did not admire his father, and as for affection, that is difficult to judge. It is known that Thomas could be harsh with his son. Lincoln's cousin and boyhood companion, Dennis Hanks, remarked that Thomas was not reluctant to give young Abe a good whipping for a variety of childish sins. He was not to ask questions of visitors, for example. For that, Thomas would give him a sharp slap across the face. Nor was he to preach to his young friends on Sunday afternoons (his stepmother said that he could repeat their minister's sermons verbatim). For that offense he would receive a dozen whacks with the paddle.

The year 1854 marked the end of the Whig Party. It was supplanted by the Republican Party, opposed to both slavery and states' rights. Lincoln was considered a leading Republican, though he was defeated for a seat in Congress by Lyman Trumbull. A few months later the Supreme Court's *Dred Scott* decision hardened Lincoln's opposition to slavery. However, he freely admitted that citizens had a constitutional right to own slaves if they chose, an opinion he never abandoned. During the Civil War he repeatedly stated that the government was fighting to preserve the union and not to abolish slavery. Indeed, at the urging of Lincoln and Andrew Johnson, Congress in July of 1861 passed the Crittenden-Johnson Resolution, which stated that the war was being waged to restore the union and not to free any slaves.

Lincoln became the Republican candidate for Illinois' U.S. Senate seat in 1858 and was opposed by Democrat Stephen Douglas, who had earlier sponsored the Kansas-Nebraska Act, which almost immediately led to bloodshed between slaveholders and non-slaveholders in those Western states. The two politicians engaged in a series of seven debates across the state. In their first debate, attended by some ten thousand citizens, Lincoln assured his audience that he recognized that the white man is far superior to the black man in every way and that he certainly had no intention of integrating the races. This was a theme he repeated in all the debates. Although he lost the election to Douglas, his name became famous throughout the country and paved the way to his being elected president just two years later.

In 1860, the Republican Party nominated Lincoln for president at its convention in Chicago, which led to his being elected president in November of that year. A few weeks later, on December 20, as a result of Lincoln's election, South Carolina seceded. With South Carolina's secession, tensions were high. U.S. major Robert Anderson hurried to occupy Fort Sumter in Charleston Harbor and refused to leave the fort when requested by Charleston authorities.

In January of 1861 a Federal ship, *Star of the West,* attempted to resupply Fort Sumter but retreated when Southern batteries opened fire. President Buchanan took no action in retaliation. Then six more states, including Texas, seceded. Representatives from those seven Southern states met in Montgomery, Alabama, the first capital of the Confederacy, to decide future policy. They did not seek war with the United States but wished only to be free of to form their own government.

On March 4, 1861, Lincoln was inaugurated as the sixteenth president of the United States and immediately took steps to force the Confederate states back into the union. The states claimed that they had a constitutional right to secede and made a very good case for themselves. Lincoln ignored their claims, and hostilities commenced little more than a month later.

On the eve of the battle for Fort Sumter, Confederate general P. G. T. Beauregard visited with his old friend and West Point professor, Maj. Robert Anderson. Anderson informed him that the fort was out of both food and water. If Beauregard would only wait forty-eight hours, said Anderson, the Southern general and his soldiers could occupy the fort without firing a shot. However, U.S. Naval ships were massing in the harbor in order to resupply the Northern soldiers.

Southern forces opened fire on Fort Sumter on April 12, 1861, and Major Anderson was forced to surrender. At that point, with Congress in recess, Lincoln became the American Napoleon, and using Fort Sumter as an excuse, started a war. Without Congress ever formally declaring war on the Confederacy, Lincoln called for an immediate and illegal blockade off the coasts of Virginia and North Carolina and requested seventy-five thousand volunteers for the United States Army. A month later he called for another five hundred thousand volunteers. In order to justify sending soldiers across state lines into Virginia, he used a series of little-known statutes, the Militia Act, passed by Congress in 1792. The statutes provided the president with the authority to call out the militia in order to put down any foreign invasion or quell uprisings. It was first invoked in 1794 when George Washington sent several hundred men into Pennsylvania to suppress the so-called Whiskey Rebellion. The situation with the Confederacy was totally different, but it was the only justification Lincoln could find for exercising martial law.

Jefferson Davis and his Confederates down in Montgomery were flabbergasted when informed that Lincoln would use the battle over Fort Sumter as a pretext for initiating a civil war. The U. S. government had constructed the fort to protect Charleston's citizens from foreign attack. Now that South Carolina was no longer a state in the union, Charleston and its citizens were no longer the responsibility of the federal government. It would seem logical that the United States would relinquish the fort, and all the expenses involved in maintaining it, to the government of South Carolina. That Lincoln insisted on going to war with the Southern states over it lends credence to those who argue that he used the fort simply as an excuse.

In July, Lincoln's Federal army met a badly outnumbered Confederate army at Manassas Junction (Bull Run) in Virginia. Before the day had ended, the Union army had been badly whipped, and some of those Northern soldiers were still running hours later when they sped by Washington, D.C. Lincoln was shattered, and apparently very surprised. Despite what he had been promised by various members of Congress and his military leaders, it would take more than one battle to end the secession problem.

The war went badly for Lincoln and the Union from First Manassas until the very end, with a few notable exceptions, despite the fact that the United States fielded the biggest and best-equipped army in the world against a ragtag army of badly outnumbered Confederates. There are several explanations for this inexplicable turn of events. Secretary of War Edwin Stanton, unscrupulous and ambitious, repeatedly appointed drunken incompetents to command his various armies. There are indications that he intentionally did so in order to prolong the war and establish himself as the most powerful man in America, thereby ensuring his election to the presidency in 1868.

There's also the matter of motivation: a great many Union soldiers were recent immigrants to America who joined the army to receive the bonus paid to recruits. These young men lacked the motivation to fight and die for the United States. They only wanted to return home as soon as possible with their pockets full of Federal money.

The Confederate armies, on the other hand, were led by the nation's foremost military leaders, such as Robert E. Lee, Stonewall Jackson, Albert Sidney Johnston, Joseph Johnston, and Jeb Stuart. As for the average Confederate soldier, he came equipped with the best motivation of all: he was fighting not for money but to protect his home and family from an invader. And he did fight. He fought tooth and nail from beginning to end, to Lincoln's consternation.

In Washington, meanwhile, spurred on by such Radicals as William Seward, a Yale-educated dandy; Edwin Stanton, with his perfumed beard; and Ben Wade, who heartily despised Lincoln, the president claimed the Militia Act of 1792 gave him the right to put down the insurrection in any manner he chose and became a handy crutch to justify his most outrageous moves. With the outbreak of war he declared martial law throughout the North. He suspended the writ of habeas corpus. Over the coming months thousands of citizens who criticized Lincoln or the war were jailed. No charges were brought against them, nor were they brought to trial. The same policy was applied to Northern newspapers. Dozens of newspapers that criticized Lincoln or his war were put out of business. In cities throughout the North, soldiers would haul the owner and editor to jail and then burn the newspaper building to the ground.

By June 15, 1861, Lincoln's actions had become so extralegal that Roger B. Taney, chief justice of the Supreme Court, sent him a written message warning that he had taken the Militia Act much too far. Not even the king of England had the authority to suspend the writ of habeas corpus, warned Taney, and certainly the president of the United States did not. That was a matter for Congress to decide. Taney concluded by warning Lincoln that his actions were clearly unconstitutional and he was in danger of impeachment by Congress should his behavior persist.

But Congress was in recess and Lincoln would not call them back into session until July 4, at which point it would be far too late for them to cancel the war for which he and the Radicals in the government had so carefully prepared since his election. Plus, with the war raging, it would be far too late to begin impeachment proceedings. He had, with the support of the Radicals in Congress, most cleverly set himself up as supreme dictator of the country. And there was nothing the Supreme Court or Congress could do about it.

One historian notes that "no study of American government should begin prior to 1861." And for good reason. Once Lincoln became president, he scrapped both the Constitution and the form of American government as Americans had known them since the days of the Founding Fathers. Heretofore, the national government had been a loose confederation of individual states, and the citizens of each state had the constitutional right to determine the laws and destiny of that state. Should it be in their best interests to secede from the union, they had a right to do so. In fact, Massachusetts had come close to seceding in 1848 over the Mexican War, which its citizens saw as the most unholy of wars.

But Lincoln's election marked the end of states' rights and constitutional government as Americans had always known it. From now on the federal government would be all powerful, while the individual states would have little power or authority to determine their own destiny. The same is true today.

Lincoln's term as president would be consumed by a war waged not for the noble purpose of freeing black Americans from bondage, as many believe, but for protecting and strengthening the role of the federal government. Many Americans, then and now, view the Civil War as little more than a fight for power on the part of Abraham Lincoln and his Republican Party. During that struggle, Lincoln became fixated on his goal of preserving the union of states, doing so at any cost.

At what point did Lincoln pass from the inspirational young

lawyer of Springfield to the warmonger president? Horace Greeley provides a reasonable explanation: "Lincoln himself is as honest as the day is long, but he has been caught up in a web spun by those unscrupulous spiders who reside in congress."

After four long, bloody years of war, America's Civil War officially ended on April 9, 1865. As Lincoln began formulating his plans for the Reconstruction of the South, plans that were considered to be far too lenient by members of his cabinet and representatives of the Radical Republican party, John Wilkes Booth, some believe with the prompting of powerful political allies, ended the president's life. On April 14, 1865, after Booth's previous plot to kidnap the president had gone awry, the actor crept into the presidential box at Ford's Theatre, where Mr. and Mrs. Lincoln were enjoying a performance of *Our American Cousin.* He fired the pistol at the back of Lincoln's head, jumped from the box, and fled across the theater stage.

Carried to a nearby boardinghouse, Lincoln died at 7:22 A.M. the morning of April 15. He left behind a nation battered and bloodied, reeling from a war that pit brother against brother, and a reinvented government founded on the sacrifices of those who believed in freedom.

A Lincoln Photo Gallery

1846. Lincoln's first photograph.

1854

1858

1859

1860. Lincoln's last photograph without a beard.   1860. Lincoln's first photograph with a beard.

1861   1863

1863

1864

1865

1865. Lincoln's last known individual photograph.

Lincoln's Family

Mary Todd Lincoln, between 1860 and 1865.

William Wallace "Willie" Lincoln, born in 1850, died at the White House in 1862. Thomas "Tad" Lincoln, at right, was born in 1852. Both boys are pictured in 1859. (Indiana State Museum)

Robert Todd Lincoln, the eldest son, born in 1843.

The Early Years:
1809-1829

Abraham Lincoln was born to Thomas and Nancy Hanks Lincoln in this one-room log cabin on the Nolan River in Hardin County, Kentucky, on February 12, 1809, a bitterly cold morning with the sleet coming down like bullets. Tom was an illiterate farmer and carpenter who married Nancy, a woman of illegitimate birth, in 1806. They had three children, Sarah, Abraham, and Tom, Jr., who died in infancy.

Nancy's mother, Lucy Hanks Sparrow, and her husband, Henry Sparrow, attended the birth. Present also was Dennis Hanks, Abraham's first cousin. Dennis was nine years Abraham's senior and also illegitimate. He would be young Lincoln's best friend growing up and would prove an invaluable source of information to Lincoln biographers.

In later years Lincoln would say that no one really knew exactly when he was born, but February 12 sounded as good as any other date. (Illinois State Historical Society)

Thomas Lincoln, whose father, Abraham, had been killed by a band of marauding Indians when Thomas was just a child. The future president bore no resemblance whatsoever to his father, who stood five feet, nine inches and weighed about 190 pounds. Reputed to be slow of both body and mind, Thomas Lincoln purportedly had suffered from a severe case of the mumps as a boy and could not father children. He was a hard-working backwoodsman and a devoted Baptist whose church forbade slavery. He was known to punish young Abraham by slapping him in the face for a variety of childish misadventures. As Lincoln grew, his relationship with his father became increasingly strained, and he did not attend his father's funeral. (Library of Congress)

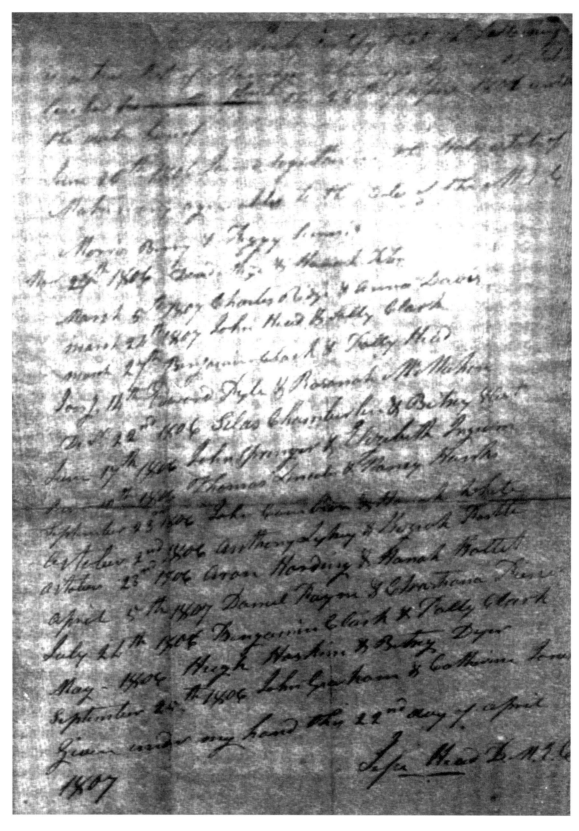

The marriage return of the Reverend Jesse Head certifying the marriage of Thomas Lincoln and Nancy Hanks, dated 1806, the same year Lincoln's older sister, Sarah, was born.

The marriage bond between Henry Sparrow and Lucy Hanks, young Lincoln's grandmother. She had once been jailed for fornication, but following her marriage to Henry Sparrow she became a respectable woman and gave birth to nine children. (This marriage bond was discovered in the courthouse in Harrodsburg, Kentucky, by Mary A. and Martha Stephenson.)

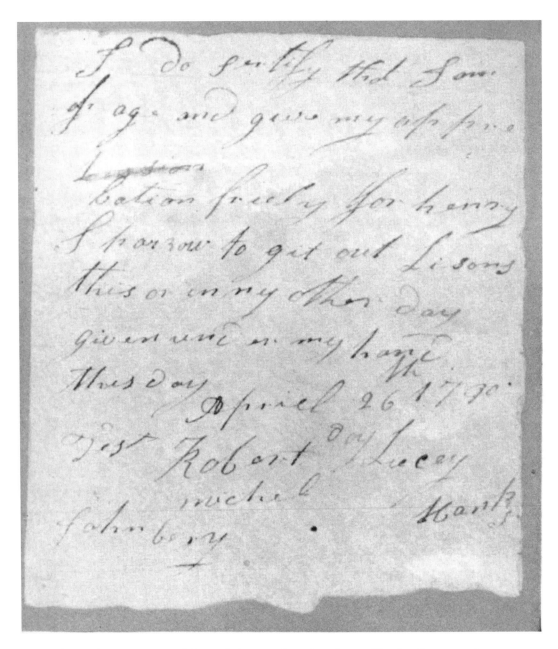

The only signature of Lincoln's grandmother Lucy Hanks Sparrow known to exist. It was discovered by Lincoln biographer William E. Barton in 1925.

Dennis Hanks, Lincoln's illegitimate first cousin and his childhood best friend. Hanks would be a storehouse of knowledge concerning his famous cousin. He revealed that Lincoln was a studious young man who never expressed interest in religion and suffered bouts of depression even as a child.

The Lincolns moved to this Knob Creek cabin when Abraham was two. His younger brother, Thomas, Jr., was born and died here. The Lincolns would remain in this location for another five years. (The Lincoln Museum)

THE

KENTUCKY PRECEPTOR,

CONTAINING

A NUMBER OF USEFUL LESSONS

FOR READING AND SPEAKING.

COMPILED FOR THE USE OF SCHOOLS.

BY A TEACHER.

Delightful task ! to rear the tender thought,
To teach the young idea how to shoot,
To pour the fresh instruction o'er the mind,
To breathe the enlivening spirit, and to fix
The generous purpose in the glowing breast.
                                    THOMPSON.

THIRD EDITION, REVISED, WITH CONSIDERABLE ADDITIONS.

COPY-RIGHT SECURED ACCORDING TO LAW.

LEXINGTON, (KY.)
PUBLISHED BY MACCOUN, TILFORD & CO.

1812.

The title page from young Lincoln's school reader in Indiana. He once said to his stepmother, "My best friend is a man who will loan me a book." By the age of ten he was reading history, philosophy, and the classics in American and British literature. Not only was he reading them, but his intelligence was such that he could quote extensively from them, to the delight of his stepmother. (Library of Congress)

In 1816 the Lincolns left Kentucky for good, settling on Little Pigeon Creek in Perry County, Indiana. Lincoln would later state that his family were Baptists and the Baptists had a strict prohibition against slavery, thus their move to Indiana, a Free State.

The grave of Nancy Hanks Lincoln, who died of the so-called milk sickness on October 5, 1818, when Lincoln was nine years old. Nancy was only twenty-six at the time of her death. She was buried in Pigeon Creek, Indiana, in a crude coffin made by Thomas and Abraham. This stone was erected years after her death.

The dreaded milk sickness also killed many of Lincoln's neighbors and relatives. Today doctors know milk sickness as brucellosis, an illness caused by cows eating the poisonous snake root plant. (The Lincoln Museum)

Sarah Bush Johnston, whom Thomas Lincoln married following his first wife's death. Sarah brought her own three children to this marriage. She was a kindly woman whom Abraham loved dearly. Illiterate herself, she did everything possible to encourage his education and took great pride in his ability to read even the classics at an early age. She said that as a small child Lincoln would return from church services on Sunday, gather smaller children around him, and then mount a stump and repeat the minister's sermon verbatim. For this sacrilege, he was sometimes whipped by his father. (Library of Congress)

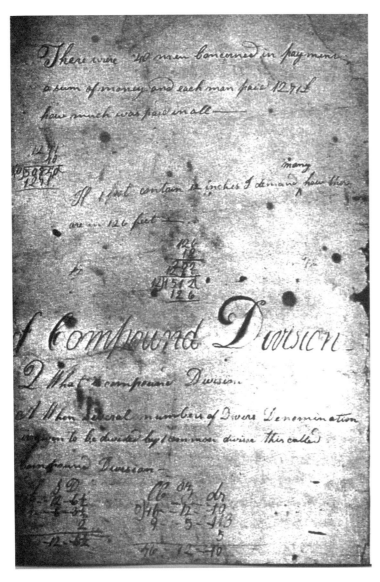

A page from Lincoln's homemade copybook. At the bottom, he wrote four lines of verse, the earliest known specimen of his handwriting. (Library of Congress)

The "blab school" kept by teacher James Swansy. At the school the students sat at their desks and read aloud, or "blabbed," to themselves until they were called on to read to the headmaster. Young Lincoln attended this school for about four months in 1822. Every morning he and his sister, Sarah, would walk two miles through the dark wilderness, braving bears, Indians, and renegade whites to receive an education. As he had been required to do at the blab school, Lincoln would develop the habit of always reading aloud to himself. (The Lincoln Museum)

The Anderson Creek ferry where Lincoln first worked away from his father's supervision. He was overjoyed to learn that working for others paid money. (Illinois State Historical Library)

Abraham Lincoln
his hand and pen
he will be good but
god knows When

An entry Lincoln scribbled in his school book in 1823, displaying for the first time the wit that would make him famous. His stepmother, Sarah Bush Lincoln, preserved it. (Library of Congress)

Lincoln's very attractive stepsister, Sarah Elizabeth Johnston, married his cousin and best friend, Dennis Hanks, when she was only fifteen. (Illinois State Historical Library)

Sarah Lincoln Grigsby, Abraham Lincoln's older sister, died in childbirth in 1828 and is buried, along with her baby, at Pigeon Creek. Abraham was devastated. (The Lincoln Museum)

As a teenager Lincoln was hired to take a flatboat loaded with produce to New Orleans to sell. While there he witnessed a slave auction, a scene that he would long remember. He was especially touched by the cries of young children being snatched from their mothers' arms.

As president, Lincoln was aware that slavery had been abolished throughout the western world without firing a shot. (Mexico was the first nation to abolish slavery.) That deed had been accomplished by the various federal governments paying slave owners to free their slaves. Throughout the Civil War, Lincoln offered to have the U.S. government pay Southern slave owners to free their slaves. There were no takers.

His Emancipation Proclamation, enacted in January 1863, freed only slaves in those areas occupied by the Confederate army, effectively freeing no slaves whatsoever. It did, however, achieve its main purpose: to keep England and France out of the war on the side of the Confederacy. (The Chicago Historical Society)

Lincoln's Paternity

Two views of Abraham Lincoln and John C. Calhoun, rumored by some to be Lincoln's father. For some two hundred years a controversy has raged concerning the identity of Lincoln's father. Was it truly Thomas Lincoln, as the record indicates, or was it John C. Calhoun, a young attorney from Abbeville, South Carolina? Local history has it that Calhoun had a sexual affair with a young barmaid, one Nancy Hanks, in a roadhouse in Anderson, South Carolina, where he frequently stayed overnight. She became pregnant, and Calhoun, hoping to avoid a scandal, paid a cattle driver named Thomas Lincoln, who was in town selling cattle, five hundred dollars to take her back to Kentucky with him. Lincoln agreed and eventually married her.

While Thomas Lincoln was in Anderson, city fathers paid him to travel to Columbia and bring back a cannon. That cannon now sits on the courthouse green in Anderson. (Library of Congress)

Two views of Abraham Lincoln and Wesley Enloe, whom local legends purports is Lincoln's half brother. Another persistent rumor has it that Lincoln was the son of Abraham Enloe, a prosperous farmer of Ocona Lufta, North Carolina. Residents of that city claim that Enloe and his wife had a young maid in their employ named Nancy Hanks. In time she and Enloe had a sexual relationship and Nancy became pregnant. The baby was said to have strongly favored old Enloe and was named Abraham after his father. Enloe's wife also noted the resemblance and flew into a rage. She ordered her husband to send Nancy Hanks and the baby away. Fortunately for Enloe, a Kentucky cattle driver named Thomas Lincoln stopped by the Enloe farm on his way home from Anderson, South Carolina. Enloe paid him to take Nancy and the baby away with him. He did so and later married her.

In the above photos we see Wesley Enloe, the son of Abraham Enloe, who, if rumors are correct, was the half brother of Abraham Lincoln. Enloe was eighty-eight years old at the time the photos were taken. (Lincoln photos from Library of Congress; Enloe photos from James Coggins, *The Eugenics of President Abraham Lincoln*)

In addition to other strikingly similar physical features, both Wesley Enloe and Lincoln stood six feet, four inches tall. (Lincoln photo from Library of Congress; Enloe photo from James Coggins, *The Eugenics of President Abraham Lincoln*)

The home of Abraham Enloe and his family in Ocona Lufta, North Carolina. It was from here that Nancy Hanks and her bastard son were sent to Kentucky in the company of Thomas Lincoln. (James Coggins, *The Eugenics of President Abraham Lincoln*)

"The true birth place of Abraham Lincoln, one mile north of Bostic, North Carolina." Only a pile of stones marks the site of the first home of Abraham Enloe, where Nancy Hanks purportedly lived when her child was born. These stones were part of the basement where the illegitimate baby was said to have been hidden when unwelcome visitors arrived. (From James Coggins, *The Eugenics of President Abraham Lincoln*)

A Light in the Wilderness:
1830-1839

Lincoln moved to Macon County, Illinois, with his family on March 1, 1830. They lived in this cabin, which he and Thomas Lincoln built with their own hands. By now Lincoln was twenty-one years old, a man. (Illinois State Historical Society)

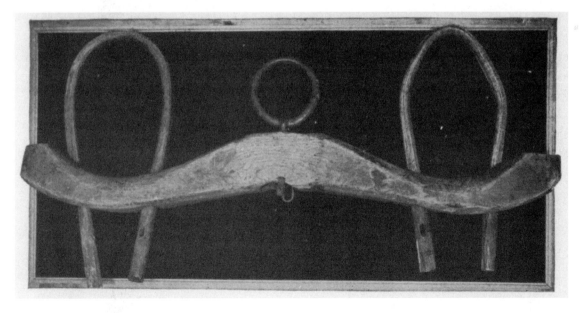

An ox yoke carved by Abraham Lincoln himself when his family decided to move to Illinois. (Illinois State Historical Society)

Lincoln the Rail Splitter by J. L. G. Ferris. (Library of Congress)

Jack Armstrong, reputed to be the strongest boy in Sangamon County, Illinois. Armstrong challenged Lincoln to a fight, one that the future president won with little effort, for despite Lincoln's slim appearance, he was extremely strong from having worked with an ax for many years. After the contest, Armstrong and his followers became Lincoln's closest friends. Throughout life Lincoln had a knack for making friends of former enemies, a talent he later displayed when he held out the olive branch to the South as the Civil War came to a close. (Illinois State Historical Society)

Lincoln's cousin John Hanks, who persuaded him to make his first political speech. Several candidates were running for public office in the area and Hanks persuaded him to stand upon a stump and speak out before a large crowd in favor of a friend. Before Lincoln had finished speaking, Hanks was amazed to find that the crowd was on its feet, applauding and yelling. From that beginning Lincoln found that he, with his sharp wit and sense of humor, had a talent for grabbing and holding an audience's attention.

In 1831, Hanks traveled down the Mississippi River with his cousin aboard a flatboat loaded with goods to sell in New Orleans. While tied up one night, the raft was attacked by five freed slaves seeking money and goods they could sell. Lincoln awakened and chased the men away with his ax. It was while in New Orleans that Lincoln first glimpsed a slave auction. Lincoln and Hanks sold their goods, sold the flatboat, and rode back to New Salem aboard a steamboat. (Illinois State Historical Library)

The Denton Offutt store in New Salem, where Lincoln worked after he left home in the spring of 1831. It was here that he gained a reputation for honesty. One evening he discovered he had overcharged a lady six cents for goods she had purchased. He walked four miles to return her money.

Bill Green, from the backwoods of Illinois, worked alongside Lincoln at the Denton Offutt store. He and Lincoln lived in the back room of the store, where they shared a narrow sleeping cot. Green later became a rich source for Lincoln biographers.

I CERTIFY, That *David M Pantier* volunteered and s... *as a private* in the Company of Mounted Volunteers und... command, in the Regiment commanded by Col. SAMUEL M. THOMPSON, in the Brigade under the ...mand of Generals S. WHITESIDE and H. ATKINSON, called into the service of the United Sta... the Commander-in-Chief of the Militia of the State, for the protection of the North Western Fr... against an Invasion of the British Band of Sac and other tribes of Indians,—that he was enrolled ... *21st* day of *April* 1832, and was HONORABLY DISCHARGED o... *7th* day of *June* thereafter, having served *48* ...

Given under my hand, this *26th* day of *September* 1...

A Lincoln

As captain of a company of Illinois volunteers in the Black Hawk War, Lincoln was responsible for discharging a recruit who had served for forty-eight days. (National Archives)

When in 1832, Black Hawk, chief of the Sauk-Fox Indians, was unable to reclaim lands he had earlier traded to the white man in Illinois, a war between the Indian nation and American settlers ensued. Lincoln spent two months as a captain in the state militia during the Black Hawk War, which he called the most rewarding experience of his life. In later years he recalled with a laugh ordering a young private to hold his horse. The private gave him a hard look and replied, "You go to hell." After almost a year's service Lincoln returned to New Salem without having fired a shot. (Library of Congress)

A reproduction of the interior of the Lincoln-Berry store. Here Lincoln spent his days reading Robert Burns and Shakespeare, while Berry whiled away his time drinking whiskey and playing poker. Berry died unexpectedly and Lincoln was saddled with debts totaling eleven hundred dollars that took him fifteen years to pay off. (Illinois State Historical Library)

The Lincoln-Berry store in New Salem, which Lincoln opened along with William F. Berry. This was Lincoln's first venture into the business world, one that lasted a very short time and left him deeply in debt. (Illinois State Historical Library)

The Rutledge Tavern in New Salem, owned and operated by James Rutledge, the father of Ann Rutledge. This tavern was the center of social activities in the little community and a place where Lincoln spent much of his free time. James Rutledge, a man of culture, began a debate and literary society in New Salem and there Lincoln quickly gained a reputation as an excellent speaker with an unusually sharp mind.

In August of 1832, at the age of twenty-three, Lincoln decided to run for the Illinois General Assembly. He lost the election but established himself as an excellent speaker and a future political force. (Library of Congress)

478   ABRAHAM LINCOLN

If A. can prove, however conclusively, that he may, of right, enslave B.— why may not B. snatch the same argument, and prove equally, that he may enslave A?—

You say A. is white, and B. is black. It is color, then; the lighter, having the right to enslave the darker? Take care— By this rule, you are to be slave to the first man you meet, with a fairer skin than your own.

You do not mean color exactly?— You mean the whites are intellectually the superior of the blacks, and, therefore have the right to enslave them? Take care again— By this rule, you are to be slave to the first man you meet, with an intellect superior to your own—

But, say you, it is a question of interest; and, if you can make it your interest, you have the right to enslave another— Very well— And if he can make it his interest, he has the right to enslave you—

Lincoln writes loose notes trying to reason in politics and human relationships with some of the absolute quality of mathematics. To *prove* a thing isn't enough; he wants to *demonstrate*. By such tests and rehearsals he aims to be trained so that he can meet all comers in debate and overthrow them. He is dropping away from the horse-play and comic sarcasm of his oratorical style of earlier years. The page reproduced above slightly reduces Lincoln's handwriting. The original is in the Barrett Collection.

Here, at the age of twenty-four in 1833, Abraham Lincoln uses irrefutable logic to prove that slavery is wrong, arguing that if you would not be a slave yourself, then you should not wish to own slaves. Throughout his adult life he would work out problems of ethics and morality much as one would a mathematical problem. One can only wonder what this young genius might have accomplished had he had the advantage of a university education. (National Archives)

In 1833, Lincoln was appointed postmaster in New Salem. He also took up land surveying. Mentor Graham (left), the New Salem schoolmaster, spent many hours teaching Lincoln the mathematical intricacies of land surveying. Lincoln caught on quickly. (National Archives)

A flat stone found by William Green, a friend of young Lincoln's, near the Lincoln-Berry store in New Salem. The chipped lettering reads: "A. Lincoln and Ann Rutledge were betrothed here July 4, 1833." Ann Rutledge, who by most accounts was simply a friend, died of malaria fever in 1835. (Oliver R. Barrett Collection)

In the summer of 1834, Lincoln broke this ax handle splitting rails for a local farmer. While waiting for a new ax to arrive, he whittled his signature, his location, and the date with his jackknife. (Oliver R. Barrett Collection)

The Illinois State House at Vandalia. In 1834, Lincoln was elected to the Illinois House of Representatives, where he would serve out four successive terms as a representative from Sangamon County. Throughout his term he would take a moderate anti-slavery position. (Illinois State Historical Society)

John Todd Stuart, Mary Todd's first cousin and a fine lawyer who encouraged Lincoln to study law, helped his future in-law open an office in Springfield. All who knew Lincoln at that time liked him and were eager to help him in any way.

Stuart was also very much aware that Lincoln was bedeviled by a deep-seated melancholia. He recalled Lincoln in the McLean County Courthouse one afternoon: "He was sitting in a corner, remote from everyone, wrapped in abstraction and gloom. I watched him for some time. He seemed to be pursuing in his mind some specific painful subject regularly and systematically through various sinuosities, and his sad face would assume, at times, deeper phases of grief. No relief came till he was roused by the adjournment of court, when he emerged from his cave of gloom, like one awakening from a deep sleep." (Illinois State Historical Society)

Joshua Fry Speed, a young merchant of Springfield who befriended Lincoln with both money and companionship in 1837. The two roomed together, sharing Speed's upstairs bed. Lincoln had just been elected to the Illinois state legislature and been admitted to the state bar, but he had little money. Thus, Speed's friendship was worth a great deal to him.

During the Civil War, Lincoln appointed Speed's brother, James Speed, to the position of attorney general, replacing Edward Bates. (Illinois State Historical Society)

In 1837, Lincoln promised a very handsome lady in Springfield that he would marry her younger sister, one Mary Owens, pictured left, if she would bring her up from Kentucky. When Mary Owens arrived, she looked nothing like her handsome sister. She was twenty-nine, stood five feet, five inches, and weighed 160 pounds. And she had not a tooth in her head. Lincoln was astounded and worked for weeks trying to convince Mary that he was not the man for her. To Lincoln's relief, she declared that she strongly disapproved of his lack of culture and ill breeding and would not marry him for anything. Below is a letter Lincoln wrote to Mary in May 1837 in an attempt to convince her not to marry him. (The Chicago Historical Society)

In 1838, Lincoln, a devoted Whig, ran for the office of presidential elector. His opponent was a Northern Democrat, Stephen Douglas, a man who would become a major opponent over the next sixteen years for a variety of public offices. Their debates became a matter of legend. Their first debate occurred at the Illinois State House in November of 1838. Called "the Little Giant," Douglas stood only five foot four but he was a fine speaker and later married a wealthy plantation owner from Mississippi. In the end Lincoln defeated Douglas for the position, while his law partner, John Todd Stuart, won a seat in Congress. Douglas would also become a competitor for the hand of Mary Todd, a battle which Lincoln won, much to his later regret. (National Archives)

Downtown Springfield in 1838, a very prosperous city with fifteen hundred
citizens. The sidewalks and roads were made of split logs, flat sides up.
Citizens complained in the local newspaper that dogs and hogs ran wild
in the streets. There were in Sangamon County at that time seventy-eight
free blacks, twenty indentured servants, and six slaves. Joshua Speed ran
a general store on the pictured block. (Illinois State Historical Society)

A Place in the Sun:
1840-1849

In 1840, Lincoln was elected to his final term in the Illinois House of Representatives and became engaged to Mary Todd. Mary was short, pudgy, and spoiled by her doting father, a Kentucky slave owner. It was said that her sharp tongue and unstable disposition had long ago chased away most of her friends. (Library of Congress)

Judge Stephen T. Logan, one of the finest lawyers in Illinois, became Lincoln's partner in 1841. (Library of Congress)

In 1841, Lincoln wrote a letter to old friend Josh Speed's sister in which he mentioned a recent steamboat trip down the Ohio River and the frivolous behavior of a dozen black slaves on board who were being sold down the river, never to see homes, friends, or relatives again. They did not seem to realize the seriousness of their situation, Lincoln wrote, but played their fiddles, sang, danced, and gambled from sunup 'til dark. He wondered what could be done for such people. (Meserve-Kunhardt Collection, Library of Congress)

Elizabeth and Ninian Edwards, Mary Todd's sister and her wealthy and politically connected husband (he had served as governor of Illinois), strongly objected to Mary Todd's engagement to the lowly Lincoln. Likely adding to their poor opinion of him, Lincoln twice left his intended standing at the altar in her sister's home before he finally convinced himself that his political future would be assured with his marriage to the spoiled and obnoxious Mary. (Illinois State Historical Library)

Mary Todd's father, the powerful and socially prominent Robert Smith Todd of Kentucky, also opposed his petted daughter's marriage to Lincoln. His sons would all become generals in the Confederate army. (Library of Congress)

Mary Todd Lincoln in her wedding dress, one her sister, Elizabeth Todd Edwards, loaned to her especially for the occasion. If friends of Lincoln are to be believed, Mary was far more happy than her fiancé about the 1842 wedding. Before her engagement, she had courted Stephen Douglas at the same time as she was seeing Lincoln. Asked which one she would marry, she replied, "The one who is most likely to become president." Her family were all Southern Democrats. (Library of Congress)

James Matheny, the clerk of court in Springfield, was a dear friend of Lincoln's and served as best man at his wedding. He would later say that, in his opinion, Lincoln was an atheist. Matheny also claimed that Lincoln was writing a book on atheism. On the afternoon of Lincoln's wedding, Matheny asked him where he was going. "To hell, I suppose," Lincoln responded sadly. (Meserve-Kunhardt Collection, Library of Congress)

The marriage license for Lincoln and Mary Todd. (Illinois State Historical Library)

The home of Ninian and Elizabeth Edwards in Springfield, located directly across the street from the Illinois State House. It was here that Lincoln married Mary Todd on November 4, 1842. (Meserve-Kunhardt Collection, Library of Congress)

The Edwards' parlor where Lincoln and Mary Todd were married. (Meserve-Kunhardt Collection, Library of Congress)

The Reverend Charles Dresser, an Episcopal minister, performed the wedding ceremony for the Lincolns. Less than two years later he would sell the couple a home in Springfield.

The Globe Tavern in Springfield was the site of the Lincolns' honeymoon and their residence during the first year of their marriage. They received a room and two meals a day for four dollars a week. It was hardly what Mary Todd's father had in mind for his daughter. (Meserve-Kunhardt Collection, Library of Congress)

Mary Todd Lincoln shortly after her wedding. (Library of Congress)

Julia Jayne, a friend who collaborated with Mary Todd on an anonymous letter published in a Springfield newspaper in 1842. In their letter, they lampooned state auditor James Shields, who was a friend of Stephen Douglas and opposed Lincoln's politics. Not only that, but he was a former suitor of Mary Todd's. Lincoln took the blame for that article. (Meserve-Kunhardt Collection, Library of Congress)

James Shields, a Democrat and the state auditor, believed that Abraham Lincoln had insulted him in the local newspaper and demanded a duel to settle the matter. When the two men met for the duel, Shields changed his mind. (Meserve-Kunhardt Collection, Library of Congress)

Lincoln purchased a home, located at Eighth and Jackson Streets in Springfield, from the Reverend Charles Dresser for fifteen hundred dollars in 1844. This photo was taken in the summer of 1860. Lincoln and his sons Willie and Tad are standing inside the fence. (Library of Congress)

William H. Herndon served as Lincoln's law partner in Springfield from 1844 until 1861 and later wrote a biography of the president. According to Herndon, Lincoln always read aloud to himself in their law office, explaining, "When I read aloud, two senses catch the idea; first I see what I read; second, I hear it, and therefore I remember it better." Herndon was a younger man at the time of his associations with Lincoln and always referred to his law partner as "Mr. Lincoln." In his biography, he recorded that Lincoln would often bring his sons to the office with him and that they would go wild, throwing books and papers from one wall to the next, dumping ash trays on the floor, and yelling out the window at passersby on the street below. "They could s—t in his hat and smear it on his shoes," wrote Herndon, "and he would just laugh and remark how clever they were." Herndon suffered from alcoholism in later life and died in poverty. (Illinois State Historical Society)

Sen. Jefferson Davis and his wife, Varina, in a photo taken only days after their 1845 wedding. Davis was a West Point graduate and a great American patriot who served in both the Black Hawk War and the Mexican War. Wife Varina was a most outspoken woman who opposed both slavery and secession, much to her husband's dismay. Davis and Lincoln would serve as presidents of their respective countries and see their countrymen torn apart by war. (Museum of the Confederacy, Richmond)

Peter Cartwright, the Jackson Democrat who opposed Lincoln for a seat in the U.S. House of Representatives in 1846. He was a hellfire and brimstone preacher famous throughout the state but he lost to Lincoln, representing the newly formed Whig party, in the election. At a church service one evening, Cartwright shouted for all who wanted to go to heaven to stand up. All rose but Lincoln. Cartwright then shouted to Lincoln, "And where do you plan to go, Mr. Lincoln?" Lincoln quietly replied, "To Congress." (McLean County Historical Society, Bloomington)

The U.S. House of Representatives in 1848. The war with Mexico consumed the legislature that year. Lincoln and the Whigs opposed the war, calling it "an unholy land grab on the part of President Polk and his cronies." The Whigs were afraid that the government might annex Texas and declare it a slave state; however, Lincoln supported the territory's right to secede. (Library of Congress)

Lincoln's best friend while serving in Congress was the senator from Georgia, Alexander Stephens, who would later serve as vice president of the Confederacy. A small man who stood less than five feet tall and weighed less than one hundred pounds, Stephens would remain dear friends with Lincoln, even throughout the Civil War. (Library of Congress)

In 1848, Pres. James Polk and Mrs. Polk posed with guests at the White House. In Congress, Abraham Lincoln, highly skeptical that America was fighting to defend American lives in Texas and Mexico, challenged Polk to identify the exact spot where American blood had been shed and thereby establish the legality of the Mexican War. From then on, the sputtering Polk avoided Lincoln whenever possible. Lincoln did, however, support the right of Texas to revolt from Mexico, stating to Congress, in words that would come back to haunt him in 1861: "Any people anywhere being inclined and having the power have the right to rise up and shake off the existing government, and form a new one that suits them better. This is a most valuable, a most sacred right—a right which we hope and believe is to liberate the world. Nor is this right confined to cases in which the whole people of an existing government may choose to exercise it. Any portion of such people, that can, may revolutionize, and make their own of so much of the territory as they inhabit." (Library of Congress)

The Wind That Swept the Nation: 1850-1859

Here lies poor Johnny Kongapod;
Have mercy on him, gracious God,
As he would do if he was God
And you were Johnny Kongapod.

Abraham Lincoln's epitaph for a Kickapoo
Indian friend in 1852. The verse demonstrates
Lincoln's clever way with words and logic.

Henry Clay, the political darling of Abraham Lincoln and the Whig Party, was three times defeated for the presidency. He ran fourth in 1824, then lost to Jackson in 1832 and to Polk in 1844. He served in public office for forty years: in the House of Representatives, as secretary of state, and as a senator from Kentucky. He founded the American Resettlement Society, an organization dedicated to sending freed slaves to Africa. Upon Clay's death in 1852, Lincoln became president of the American Resettlement Society and continued that work throughout the Civil War.

Lincoln was asked to deliver Clay's eulogy in Springfield, which he reluctantly agreed to do. He admired Clay from a political standpoint but had little use for him personally, feeling that Clay was little more than a self-serving tyrant. (Library of Congress)

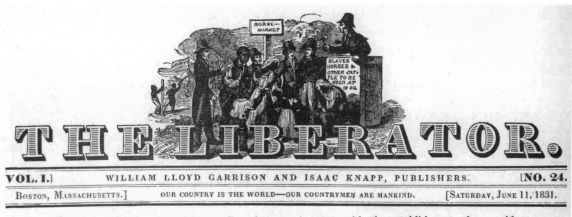

The anti-slavery movement got well under way in 1832, with the establishment of a weekly

The abolitionist movement got well underway in 1832 with the establishment of a weekly newspaper called *The Liberator,* founded and edited by William Lloyd Garrison. This publication was dedicated to recording the evils of slavery and continued publication until the end of the Civil War. It was one of several such newspapers that flourished in the North during the 1850s as abolitionist sentiment increased. (National Archives)

William Lloyd Garrison devoted his life to *The Liberator* and the abolition of slavery. Rank and file citizens of Massachusetts heartily despised him, while few Southerners had ever heard of him. (Library of Congress)

Harriet Beecher Stowe, a staunch abolitionist and the author of *Uncle Tom's Cabin.* The sister of famous minister and abolitionist Henry Ward Beecher, she was the lady, said Lincoln, who started the Civil War. (The Harriet Beecher Stowe Center)

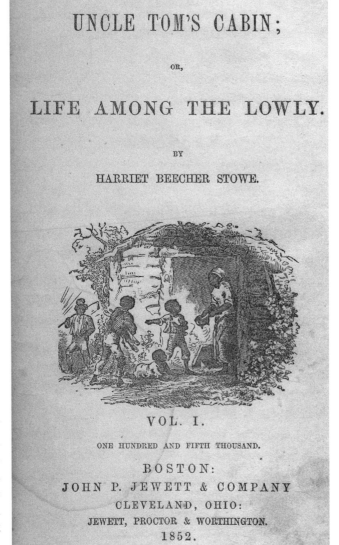

Uncle Tom's Cabin, published in 1852, was second only to the Bible as the best-selling book of the nineteenth century. An anti-slavery novel, it so impacted attitudes toward African Americans and slavery that it intensified the conflict between North and South that led to the Civil War. Ironically, the villain of this work, the cruel Simon Legree, is a transplanted Yankee. (The Harriet Beecher Stowe Center)

Caroline Lee Hentz, a native of Connecticut who married a Southern slave owner, wrote *A Planter's Northern Bride* in reply to *Uncle Tom's Cabin.* Hentz's novel claimed that slavery was a benevolent institution and a blessing to black Africans who were now able to become Christians. She and Harriet Beecher Stowe had once been close friends. (National Archives)

This illustration from *A Planter's Northern Bride* (published in Buffalo, New York) presents a defense of slavery by depicting slaves as well cared for and provided both academic and religious instruction on a regular basis. (National Archives)

Henry Ward Beecher, the brother of Harriet Beecher Stowe and for forty yeas the pastor of the Plymouth Congregational Church in Brooklyn, New York. He was a rabid abolitionist and reputed to be the most well-known minister of his generation. Despite his public support for the man, he suspected that Lincoln was only paying lip service to the abolitionists with his talks of freeing the slaves. (The Harriet Beecher Stowe Center)

Lincoln in 1854 while campaigning for office. Although he had been working the legal circuit in Illinois, Lincoln returned to politics in the same year the Kansas-Nebraska Act allowed settlers in those two territories to decide for themselves whether they would legalize slavery. He ran and was elected to the Illinois House of Representatives but declined the position so that he could campaign for a U.S. Senate seat. In 1855, the Illinois legislature chose Lyman Trumbull as senator. (Library of Congress)

Dred Scott became the subject of lawsuits throughout the country when he claimed he was no longer a slave because he had moved with his owner to a Free State. His case finally was heard by the Supreme Court, which ruled against him in 1857. Lincoln and others were made furious by the court's decision. (Meserve-Kunhardt Collection, Library of Congress)

John Brown and four of his sons, dedicated abolitionists all, in 1856 attacked and murdered with broadswords three Kansas slave owners. A large reward was offered for their capture, dead or alive. However, in many Northern states the Browns were regarded as heroes. In 1858, when Brown returned to Kansas, he shaved off his beard and used an alias, Shubel Morgan.

Once he returned to his home in northern New York, he began to plan the raid of a government arsenal at Harpers Ferry, Virginia, to obtain firearms for an uprising of black slaves. With the support of this black army, he hoped to establish a new nation in the Appalachian Mountains, with himself as king. Brown was captured by troops commanded by Robert E. Lee, found guilty of treason, and hanged at Charlestown, Virginia, on December 2, 1859. His death gave the abolitionists a martyr for their cause. Lincoln's comment on the raid was typical: "John Brown was no Republican." (Boston Athenaeum)

Nominated as a Republican for the U.S. Senate, Lincoln challenged the Democratic Stephen Douglas to seven debates. The Lincoln-Douglas debates of 1858 are recalled as the greatest political debates in history. Some drew as many as ten thousand citizens. (Illinois State Historical Library)

The Lincoln-Douglas debates centered around the slavery question. Lincoln stated that slavery should be forbidden in the western territories, while Douglas, who had sponsored the Kansas-Nebraska Act, supported the Squatter-Sovereignty Plan of letting the citizens of the various western territories decide the issue for themselves. The clever Lincoln soon maneuvered the debates into a discussion of whether slavery was right or wrong. Douglas's comments infuriated the South and likely cost him the presidency. (Library of Congress)

The seven Lincoln-Douglas debates during the late summer and early fall of 1858 were the highlight of the campaign for Illinois's U.S. Senate seat. Ten thousand people attended the opening three-hour debate in Ottawa, Illinois, and there were fifteen thousand at the second in Freeport. Audiences were treated to the greatest public debates in the history of America. During his debates with Douglas, Lincoln repeatedly stated his position on race: "I have no purpose to introduce political and social equality between the white and black races. There is a physical difference between the two, which, in my judgment, will probably forever forbid their living together upon the footing of perfect equality; and inasmuch as it becomes a necessity that there must be a difference, I, as well as Judge Douglas, am in favor of the race to which I belong having the superior position. I have never said anything to the contrary."

Lincoln received sixteen thousand more votes than Douglas in the election, but in 1858 senators were elected by the U.S. Senate and thus the election went to Douglas.

In this photograph, Lincoln's "lazy" left eye can clearly be seen. However, these debates set Lincoln on the path to the presidency. (Library of Congress)

Darkness Descends:
1860-1865

1860

Lincoln in 1860. The newly formed Republican Party was searching for a viable candidate to represent the party in the coming presidential election. Though he had not served in elected office for a decade, Lincoln had gained fame and appeal as a result of his recent series of debates with Stephen Douglas. One of five candidates campaigning for the Republican nomination, Lincoln was initially considered to have little hope of receiving the nomination. (Library of Congress)

I was born Feb. 12, 1809, in Hardin county, Kentucky. My parents were both born in Virginia, of undistinguished families — second families, perhaps I should say. My mother, who died in my tenth year, was of a family of the name of Hanks, some of whom now reside in Adams, some others in Macon counties, Illinois. My paternal grandfather, Abraham Lincoln, emigrated from Rockingham County, Virginia, to Kentucky, about 1781 or 2, where, a year or two later, he was killed by indians, not in battle, but by stealth, when he was laboring to open a farm in the forest — His ancestors, who were quakers, went to Virginia from Berks County, Pennsylvania. An effort to identify them with the New England family of the same name ended in nothing more definite, than a similarity of christian names in both families, such as Enoch, Levi, Mordecai, Solomon, Abraham, and the like —

My father, at the death of his father, was but six years of age; and he grew up, litterally without education. He removed from Kentucky to what is now Spencer county, Indiana, in my eighth year. We reached our new home about the time the State came into the Union. It was a wild region, with many bears and other wild animals still in the woods. There I grew up. There were some schools, so called; but no qualification was ever required of a teacher, beyond "readin, writin, and cipherin" to the Rule of Three. If a straggler supposed to understand latin, happened to sojourn in

Lincoln's handwritten autobiography.

the neighborhood, he was looked upon as a
wizzard— There was absolutely nothing to excite
ambition for education. Of course when I came of
age I did not know much. Still somehow I could
read, write, and cipher to the Rule of Three; but
that was all. I have not been to school since.
The little advance I now have upon this store of education, I have picked up from time to time under
the pressure of necessity—

I was raised to farm work, which I continued
till I was twenty-two— At twenty-one I came to
Illinois, and passed the first year in Illinois—
Macon county— Then I got to New-Salem (at that time
in Sangamon, now in Menard county), where I remained a year as a sort of Clerk in a
store— Then came the Black-Hawk war;
and I was elected a Captain of Volunteers—
a success which gave me more pleasure
than any I have had since— I went the
campaign, was elated, ran for the Legislature the
same year (1832), and was beaten—the only time
I ever have been beaten by the people. The next,
and three succeeding biennial elections, I was elected
on to the Legislature— I was not a candidate
afterwards. During this Legislative period I had
studied law, and removed to Springfield to
practice it— In 1846 I was once elected
to the lower House of Congress— Was not a candidate for re-election— From 1849 to 1854, both

Lincoln's handwritten autobiography, continued.

inclusion, practiced law more assiduously than ever before. Always a whig in politics, and generally on the whig electoral tickets, making active canvasses. I was losing interest in politics, when the repeal of the Missouri Compromise aroused me again. What I have done since then is pretty well known.

If any personal description of me is thought desirable, it may be said, I am, in height, six feet, four inches, nearly; lean in flesh, weighing, on an average, one hundred and eighty pounds; dark complexion, with coarse black hair, and grey eyes. No other marks or brands recollected.

Hon. J. W. Fell.   *Yours very truly*
                                           A. Lincoln

At the behest of Jesse W. Fell, a political biographer in the employ of the Republican Party, Lincoln reluctantly compiled this handwritten autobiography in December of 1859. He never liked to discuss his ancestry or his early life, so kept the biography to a minimum. He sent Fell a self-effacing note along with his brief biography:

> Here is a little sketch, as you requested. There is not much of it, for the reason, I suppose, that there is not much of me. If anything is made out of it, I wish it to be modest and not go beyond the material. If it were thought necessary to incorporate anything from my speeches, I suppose there would be no objection. Of course it must not appear to have been written by myself.

This brief life story was printed in February 1860, in the third person, and was the basis of the many campaign biographies that soon appeared. (Library of Congress)

The Wigwam in Chicago, built to house the 1860 Republican National Convention, was a two-story building that could hold ten thousand people. The convention was so crowded that many were not able to find a way inside and had to wait outside to hear the results. After three votes, Lincoln was elected the Republican nominee and the party chose as one of its platforms to end the expansion of slavery. (Chicago Historical Society)

Judge David Davis, a native of Springfield and an Eighth Circuit legal companion of Lincoln's, headed a small group of lawyers who worked to persuade delegates to the convention to support Abraham Lincoln. Their headquarters was a two-room apartment at the Tremont Hotel in Chicago, and from there Davis worked around the clock to secure Lincoln's nomination, playing a substantial role in the convention's outcome. (Library of Congress)

This poster, depicting both Lincoln and his choice for vice president, Hannibal Hamlin of Maine, informed voters that Republicans had a real chance to win the election of 1860. Rumor in Washington had it that Hamlin opposed slavery because he was part black himself. Lincoln dumped him as vice president in 1864 because of his radical views against slavery. (Meserve-Kunhardt Collection, Library of Congress)

On the morning of August 8, 1860, thousands of Republicans from all over Illinois gathered in Springfield for a large Republican rally. Excited over Lincoln's nomination as the Republican candidate, hundreds of fans surrounded the Lincoln home while exuberant citizens streamed by the house in a parade that took eight hours to pass. To the right of the doorway is Lincoln in his white suit. Mary Todd Lincoln peeks out the window on the far left, while Willie, still shaky from a bout with scarlet fever, watches from the second-floor window second from the left. The thirty-three young ladies dressed in white seated in the wagon represent the thirty-three states. Riding in a buggy are Kansas followers hoping their territory will become state number thirty-four. (Library of Congress)

A closeup of the previous picture shows Lincoln standing just to the right of his doorway, towering over his well-wishers. (Library of Congress)

On October 18, 1860, Lincoln received the following letter from a young lady named Grace Bedell who complained that he needed a beard.

Dear Sir

My father has just come home from the fair and brought home your picture and Mr. Hamlin's. I am a little girl only eleven years old, but want you should be President of the United States very much so I hope you wont think me very bold to write to such a great man as you are. Have you any little girls about as large as I am if so give them my love and tell her to write to me if you cannot answer this letter. I have got 4 brother's [sic] and part of them will vote for you any way and if you let your whiskers grow I will try and get the rest of them to vote for you you [sic] would look a great deal better for your face is so thin. All the ladies like whiskers and they would tease their husband's [sic] to vote for you and then you would be President. My father is going to vote for you and if I was a man I would vote for you to but I will try and get every one to vote for you that I can. . . .

Good bye
Grace Bedell

In response, Lincoln wrote to Miss Bedell:

My dear little Miss

Your very agreeable letter of the 15th is received. I regret the necessity of saying I have no daughters. I have three sons—one seventeen, one nine, and one seven years of age. They, with their mother, constitute my whole family. As to the whiskers, having never worn any, do you not think people would call it a piece of silly affectation if I were to begin it now?

Your very sincere well wisher
A. Lincoln

A beardless Lincoln in October of 1860. (Library of Congress)

Several weeks later, Lincoln had grown a beard. Whether Miss Bedell prompted this "silly affection" is not known. (Library of Congress)

John Cabell Breckinridge, America's fourteenth vice president and the youngest of the four candidates for president in 1860, had been a lawyer in Kentucky, a major in the Mexican War, and a member of Congress. He was serving as vice president under Buchanan when he was nominated for president. In the election, running as a Southern Democrat, he carried eleven of the Southern states, including Delaware and Maryland, receiving a total of 849,781 votes. Had Breckinridge and Douglas not split the Democratic ticket, one of them likely could have defeated Lincoln for the presidency. Following the firing on Fort Sumter, Breckinridge became a general in the Confederate army and in the final days of the war served as secretary of war under Jefferson Davis. (Museum of the Confederacy, Richmond)

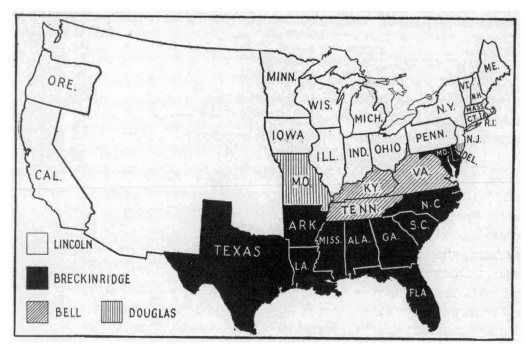

How the states voted in 1860. All the states in the North and far West were carried by Lincoln. All the states in the Deep South, plus Maryland and Delaware, went for Breckinridge. John Bell and Edward Everett (who delivered the keynote speech preceding Lincoln's Gettysburg address), running on the Constitutional Union ticket, won in three states: Virginia, Kentucky, and Tennessee. Stephen Douglas carried only Missouri.

Pres. James Buchanan and his cabinet of 1860: Lewis Cass, secretary of state; Howell Cobb, secretary of the treasury; John B. Floyd, secretary of war; Isaac Touey, secretary of the navy; Jacob Thompson, secretary of the interior; Joseph Holt, postmaster general. Within months several of these gentlemen would resign to accept positions with the government of the Confederate States of America. (Library of Congress)

This extremely rare photograph shows the South Carolina Secession Convention at work at Secession Hall in Charleston on the morning of December 20, 1861. At noon the convention issued a statement that read, "We the people of the state of South Carolina, in Convention assembled, do declare and ordain that the union now subsisting between South Carolina and other States under the name of The United States of America is hereby dissolved." In making their decision to secede, the delegates to the Secession Convention quoted the Tenth Amendment to the U.S. Constitution: "The powers not delegated to the United States by the Constitution, nor prohibited by it to the States, are reserved to the States respectively." In quick order six other states—Mississippi, Florida, Alabama, Georgia, Louisiana, and Texas—followed South Carolina out of the union. (Note the gay Christmas decorations in the hall.) (West Point Museum, United State Military Academy)

CHARLESTON

MERCURY

EXTRA:

Passed unanimously at 1.15 o'clock, P. M. December 20th, 1860.

AN ORDINANCE

To dissolve the Union between the State of South Carolina and other States united with her under the compact entitled " The Constitution of the United States of America."

We, the People of the State of South Carolina, in Convention assembled, do declare and ordain, and it is hereby declared and ordained,

That the Ordinance adopted by us in Convention, on the twenty-third day of May, in the year of our Lord one thousand seven hundred and eighty-eight, whereby the Constitution of the United States of America was ratified, and also, all Acts and parts of Acts of the General Assembly of this State, ratifying amendments of the said Constitution, are hereby repealed; and that the union now subsisting between South Carolina and other States, under the name of " The United States of America," is hereby dissolved.

THE

UNION IS DISSOLVED!

Here the *Charleston Mercury* announces South Carolina's secession. Not even the most radical among the delegates at the convention dreamed that secession would lead to war. (Library of Congress)

1861

Two of Lincoln's dearest friends, Ward Hall Lamon and Col. Elmer Ellsworth, made the long train ride from Springfield to Washington with him in February of 1861, serving as both companions and bodyguards. Lamon would remain with him as his personal secretary throughout his presidency, while Ellsworth would be killed in the opening days of the war when he attempted to pull down a Confederate flag from atop a hotel in Alexandria, Virginia. (Library of Congress)

Lincoln's wife and sons Willie and Tad the day following their arrival in Washington in February. Mary was in her glory and lorded her newfound fame over her acquaintances, much to Lincoln's chagrin. Her minister back in Springfield said metal barrel hoops should be put around her to keep her from exploding. Note that Willie, who would die in 1862, had already been taught to pose for the camera. (Library of Congress)

Thousands of citizens gathered in front of the unfinished Capitol to witness Lincoln's first inauguration on March 4, 1861, when he stated for all to hear that American citizens had a constitutional right to own slaves. Still, the Southern states seceded from the union, proving that there was more to their decision to secede than the question of slavery. Southerners were particularly concerned with states' rights and constitutional government as it had been known in America since the days of the Founding Fathers. Lincoln, a Republican, had been a Whig until that party dissolved in 1856. His political philosophies had not changed with the demise of the Whig party, and it had been the goal of the Whigs to form a strong centralized federal government. Such a government was imperative for Lincoln to implement his economic goals for America.

One historian has suggested that no study of American government should begin prior to 1861, for it was then that constitutional government as advocated by Thomas Jefferson was scrapped in favor of a strong centralized federal government as advocated by Alexander Hamilton. (Library of Congress)

Mary Todd Lincoln dressed for her husband's inauguration ball, a celebration that Southern sympathizers across Washington snubbed. She was supremely happy with her position as America's first lady. In time she would nearly bankrupt the office of the president with her lavish spending. (Library of Congress)

This photograph of Lincoln and his two private secretaries was taken at the home of John G. Nicolay (seated left) in Springfield just before all three departed for Washington. John Hay, standing, later served as secretary of state under both Presidents William McKinley and Theodore Roosevelt and was responsible for the open door policy with China.

In time Mary Lincoln would become insanely jealous of Nicolay and Hay, charging that Lincoln spent far more time with them in the evenings than he did with her. The two men would later collaborate on a biography of Lincoln. (National Archives)

THE COAT OF ARMS OF THE INDEPENDENT STATE OF SOUTH CAROLINA
At the left is the Latin inscription: "Prepared in Spirit and Wealth." At the right: "While I breathe I hope."

The seal of the state of South Carolina in 1860, prior to secession. (*Harper's Weekly,* 1861)

Charleston, South Carolina, in 1861. (Library of Congress)

Against orders, Maj. Robert Anderson, a Virginian by birth, had occupied Fort Sumter in late December 1860, precipitating the Civil War, during which conflict some three million Americans would die. Here Anderson is pictured with his wife, Eliza, and son, Robert, Jr.

Lincoln's first cabinet meetings were dominated by discussions of what to do about Fort Sumter, in Charleston harbor. The federal government weighed two options: to simply withdraw the 127 soldiers under Maj. Robert Anderson or to reinforce the garrison, thereby initiating a war with the Southern states. Although only one of Lincoln's cabinet members advocated reinforcing the fort, Lincoln opted to fight for its reclamation, thereby unleashing the most devastating episode in this nation's history. (Library of Congress)

Secretary of State William H. Seward of New York. To Seward's great disappointment, Lincoln denied him permission to meet with the South Carolina emissaries who came to negotiate the purchase of Fort Sumter. The result was war, which Seward opposed. (Library of Congress)

Fort Sumter in the early-morning hours of April 12, 1861. After two days of constant shelling from surrounding cannon batteries, Maj. Robert Anderson surrendered the fort to the South Carolina militia. Neither side experienced a single casualty. Indeed, after much hand shaking and back slapping among old friends from the two sides, the Northern officers and soldiers were fed a fine meal then escorted to a waiting ship and returned home. (Library of Congress)

General in chief of the U.S. Army in 1860, Winfield Scott warned Lincoln that it would take twenty-five thousand soldiers six months to capture Fort Sumter from the Confederates. (National Archives)

Gen. P. G. T. Beauregard served as superintendent at West Point prior to the war, then commanded Southern forces in Charleston during the attack on Fort Sumter. Later he would share command with Joe Johnston of forces at First Manassas. (Library of Congress)

Following the fall of Fort Sumter the city of Charleston depended for its safety upon a ring of fortified artillery positioned around the city. Pictured is the Laurens Street Battery in downtown Charleston. Such batteries would keep Union forces at bay until the final days of the war. Battered Fort Sumter can be seen in the background, a Confederate flag flying overhead. (Museum of the Confederacy, Richmond)

Chief Justice Roger B. Taney. Lincoln used the Militia Act of 1792, first invoked by George Washington to suppress the Whiskey Rebellion, to justify sending troops across state lines into Virginia. Chief Justice Taney wrote Lincoln an official letter in which he informed him that the Militia Act was no excuse for the unconstitutional actions being taken by the government, for the president had also declared martial law in the North and suspended the writ of habeas corpus. Not even the king of England had the authority to suspend the writ of habeas corpus, said Taney. Lincoln must cease such acts immediately, warned the chief justice, or he would stand in danger of impeachment. With Congress in recess until July 4, Lincoln, at the urging of the Radical Republicans who surrounded him, ignored Taney's warning and continued his illegal actions. (National Archives)

Thad Stevens, a Radical senator from Pennsylvania, brooded over not receiving the Republican nomination for president. He despised Lincoln and lost no opportunity to criticize and misguide him. He was among those Radicals who constantly badgered Lincoln into taking extreme measures that were both illegal and unconstitutional. (Library of Congress)

Jefferson Davis, a graduate of West Point, veteran of the Mexican War, U.S. senator from Mississippi, and secretary of war under Pres. Franklin Pierce. When the Southern states seceded, he wished to become a general in the Confederate army but was elected president. As president of the Confederacy, he made every effort to placate the U.S. government concerning Fort Sumter, even offering to purchase it. He was flabbergasted when Lincoln used Fort Sumter as a pretext for going to war with the Southern states. A war with the United States was the last thing the Confederacy wanted. (Library of Congress)

This extremely rare photograph shows the Alabama State House in Montgomery, the initial capital of the Confederacy, during Jefferson Davis's inauguration as president of the Confederate States of America on March 4, 1861. (The clock indicates that it is 1 P.M.) At that point only seven states had seceded. Following the firing on Fort Sumter four more followed. Four others—Delaware, Maryland, Kentucky, and Missouri—would attempt to secede but were kept in the union by force. (Library of Congress)

On April 19, 1861, Baltimore citizens, outraged at being forcibly denied the right to secede, attacked the Sixth Massachusetts Infantry when the soldiers attempted to pass through the city on their way to Washington. Four soldiers and nine civilians were killed in the fighting. As the war roared on, Maryland furnished far more troops to the Confederacy than to the Union. (American Heritage Picture Collection, New York City)

On May 24, Colonel Ellsworth pulled down a Confederate flag from atop a hotel in Alexandria, Virginia. The owner of the hotel, who had done nothing to incite an invasion of his private property, fired in self-defense, killing Ellsworth instantly. His death caused Lincoln a day of weeping. (Chicago Historical Society)

The handsome Elmer Ellsworth, Lincoln's friend from Springfield, enlisted as a colonel in the Union army. (Meserve-Kunhardt Collection, Library of Congress)

Sen. Ben Wade of Ohio, a leading Radical, despised Lincoln and stated that the president's war and slave policies were "murdering the nation." (National Archives)

On June 3, 1861, Lincoln was saddened to learn that his old antagonist, Stephen Douglas, had died suddenly of acute rheumatism. June 3, coincidentally, was the birthday of Jefferson Davis. (Library of Congress)

At Lincoln's urging, Sen. John J. Crittenden of Kentucky, along with Sen. Andrew Johnson of Tennessee, who would succeed Lincoln as president, cosponsored the Crittenden-Johnson Resolution, which stated that the war was being waged not to free the slaves but to restore the union. It passed by a large margin on July 25, 1861. It was hoped that this resolution would persuade the Border States not to secede.

Crittenden was married to Maria Todd, Mary Todd Lincoln's aunt. One of his brothers served as a general with the Union army, the other as a general with the Confederate army. (Library of Congress)

Gen. Joe Johnston commanded the Confederate army during the first year of the war. He and Gen. P. G. T. Beauregard led Confederate forces at the war's first major battle, First Manassas (Bull Run), in July of 1861, nearly destroyed the vastly superior Union army. Thereafter, Johnson was at odds with Jefferson Davis, whom he blamed for supplies not arriving on time for the battle.

In May of 1862, Johnston was wounded and Gen. Robert E. Lee was given command of Confederate forces. Upon his recovery, Johnston assumed command of the Western theater.

When Johnston surrendered his army to Sherman in April of 1865, Sherman made him such generous terms that Edwin Stanton accused the Union general of treason. A humiliated Sherman was forced to renegotiate his terms with Johnston a week later.

Johnston and Sherman had been lifelong friends, and in 1892 Johnston would serve as a pallbearer at Sherman's funeral. On that occasion Johnston stood uncovered for hours in the sleet and snow, then came down with pneumonia and died two weeks later. Offered a hat to shield him from the icy rain, Johnston had responded, "It's the least I can do for poor General Sherman. He would have done the same for me." (National Archives)

The Sumter Light Guards, a Georgia infantry regiment, holds drills in Augusta in April of 1861, proudly bearing aloft their new Stars and Bars flag. Soon these young patriots would be on their way to northern Virginia to meet the Union army at a place called Manassas Junction.

Band members in this photo (second row) appear to be African American. (Georgia Department of Archives and History)

Patriotic zeal was at a fever pitch in the North as well as in the South.
Here the Seventh New York Regiment marches down Broadway. Soon
these young patriots would be on their way to northern Virginia.
(National Archives)

The immortal Gen. Thomas "Stonewall" Jackson received his nickname at First Manassas from Gen. Bernard Bee, a South Carolinian, who shouted to his men, "Look at Jackson. He's standing like a stone wall." Jackson was a West Point graduate who performed brilliantly in the Mexican War and was serving as a professor of natural history at Virginia Military Institute when the Civil War broke out. He was killed at Chancellorsville in May of 1863 at the age of thirty-seven by his own soldiers. He has been called the greatest field general in the history of the western world. With his dying words he called on Gen. A. P. Hill to immediately come up on his left flank. (Library of Congress)

The day following the First Battle of Manassas, Confederate officers surveyed the terrible carnage. It was a tremendous victory for the South, one that taught Lincoln that the Union could not win the war in just one major battle. In fact, the war would drag on for four long, agonizing years and would cost the lives of several millions of Americans.

It should be noted that photographers traveling with the Union army rarely photographed Union dead, preferring to photograph Confederate dead. (National Archives)

After his loss at First Manassas, Gen. Irvin McDowell, Lincoln's first commander of the Army of the Potomac, ponders what went wrong with his grand plan to smash Joe Johnston's ragtag Southern rebels with his massive Union force. (Library of Congress)

Several Northern congressmen who favored war with the South assured Lincoln that the Confederates would tuck tail and run at the first shots. An undecided Lincoln made the mistake of listening to them. In fact, following the First Battle of Manassas brave young men from throughout the Confederacy rushed to join with their local infantry and cavalry units to turn back the invading Yankees. This print captures well family attitudes that were present in home after home as a young son (now a cavalry officer) rides off to join his unit in Tennessee or northern Virginia. Chances were he would never return, as the mother in this print well knows. (The Missouri State Historical Gallery)

Gen. George B. McClellan and wife, Elizabeth. Following the Union disaster at First Manassas, Lincoln reluctantly replaced the humiliated General McDowell with George McClellan, who at that point had only a single victory in West Virginia. He was made commander of the Army of the Potomac, a huge mistake for Lincoln and the Union. Fearful of General Lee's army and extremely timid, despite the fact that his army outnumbered Lee's 3 to 1, he refused to confront the enemy. He did fight Lee to a draw at Antietam but then failed to go in pursuit, leading to his dismissal. In 1864 the Democrats nominated him for president but he lost by a large margin to Lincoln. (National Archives)

THE EAGLE'S NEST.

On August 17, 1861, *Harper's Weekly* featured a fictitious print of Confederate soldiers bayoneting Union wounded at First Manassas. The caption read: "Those savages who fought under the Confederate flag systematically butchered the wounded, and this not only in obedience to their own fiendish instincts, but by order of their officers." Cries of outrage against those heathen Southerners rang throughout the North, giving rise to such patriotic posters as this one. It also led to the abuse of Southern POWs in Northern prison camps. (National Archives)

Patriotism was extremely high in the North, especially in the early, more innocent days of the conflict, with many men feeling that they were fighting a holy crusade to save America. In the above print, *The Consecration,* a handsome Union officer prepares to leave for the front while his beautiful wife blesses him by kissing his sword.

Citizens in the North were hardly touched by the war since most of the battles were fought in the South. Southern citizens, on the other hand, suffered terribly.

Gen. Phil Sheridan, Lincoln's newly appointed Potomac cavalry commander, a diminutive man in his early thirties. In the war's final year, then unopposed by Confederate forces, he roamed the Shenandoah Valley at will. His war crimes against the women and children of that area are a matter of legend. (Library of Congress)

A former explorer and later presidential candidate, Gen. John C. Frémont refused to take orders from anyone, including President Lincoln. In August 1861, he freed the slaves of Southern sympathizers in Missouri, a Border State that Lincoln was trying to hold in the Union. When Lincoln was informed of Frémont's move he became speechless with anger. When the general refused to revise his proclamation, he was dismissed as commander of the Missouri theater. He and his sympathizers lobbied Lincoln throughout the war to restore his generalship—without success. (Library of Congress)

1862

WILLIE LINCOLN, THIRD SON OF PRESIDENT LINCOLN.
DIED FEBRUARY 20, 1862, AT THE AGE OF 12.
From a photograph taken by Brady at Washington, shortly
before the death of Willie Lincoln.

Gen. Simon Bolivar Buckner, of the Confederate army. On February 16, 1862, Buckner surrendered Fort Donelson in Tennessee and surrendered fifteen thousand Confederate troops to Gen. Ulysses S. Grant, marking the Union's first major victory of the war.

Buckner and Grant had been close friends prior to the war and on one occasion Buckner had loaned Grant a great deal of money, thereby saving his reputation and his military career. However, at Fort Donelson, Grant would agree only to unconditional surrender, infuriating Buckner. Later that day, Buckner was standing at the railing of the boat taking him north when Grant approached the dock. He sent up a written message to the general that read: "I know you are far from home and friends and perhaps you are in need money. If so, my wallet is open to you." Buckner read the note, tore it to shreds, and turned away. Soon he would be exchanged. (Library of Congress)

In early February of 1862, Willie Lincoln, age eleven, was stricken with typhoid fever. He died on February 20, leaving both his parents distraught. For days Lincoln walked the hallways of the White House, his head buried in his hands, weeping for his lost son. Mary Todd, in her grief, would hire a spiritual medium who would hold séances at the White House, some attended by Lincoln himself. Asked if he believed in séances, Lincoln simply shrugged. (Library of Congress)

Following the tragic death of Willie, the Lincolns focused their attention on their third son, young Tad. When not engaged in official business, Lincoln's constant companion was Tad. He was slow mentally and was born with a cleft pallet. Only Lincoln, it was said, could understand his son's speech. Some have said that here Lincoln is reading the Bible to his son. In reality they are both perusing a Matthew Brady photo album. (Library of Congress)

Thomas "Tad" Lincoln, 1853-1871. Because of his large head and small body, he looked like a tadpole, said his father, and thus he called him Tad. (Library of Congress)

Gen. Robert E. Lee in a photograph taken the day he returned to his home in Arlington after the war. Pictured with him is his son, Gen. George Washington Custis "Boo" Lee, and his personal secretary. Gen. Lee has been called the most brilliant strategist in the history of the western world. Though vastly outnumbered, he fought the Union army to a standstill for four long years and won the admiration of Southerners and Northerners alike. Following the war he was named president of Washington College (Washington and Lee University). Gen. Boo Lee was a heroic cavalry leader with the Army of Northern Virginia throughout the war and later succeeded his father as president of Washington College.

Like Stonewall Jackson, legend has it that with his dying words Lee called on Gen. A. P. Hill to come up on Jackson's left flank. (Valentine Museum, Richmond)

Three future generals for the Confederacy upon their graduation from West Point in 1858: Stephen Dill Lee, Jeb Stuart, and George Washington Custis "Boo" Lee (the son of Robert E. Lee). Stuart was expelled from West Point on three different occasions for insubordination (fighting with upperclassmen), but he was reinstated on each occasion because of his "extreme youthfulness." (Valentine Museum, Richmond)

The elusive Jeb Stuart, one of the Confederate's finest cavalry leaders. He suffered a fatal wound to the abdomen at Yellow Tavern on May 12, 1864, when he was only twenty-eight years old. Bleeding internally, he was taken to the home of a relative in Richmond to await the end. As he lay dying he asked the assembled friends and relatives to sing "Rock of Ages," his favorite song. Then he passed quietly away. (Valentine Museum, Richmond)

Despite being married, Stuart carried on a torrid love affair with a beautiful nurse at the Confederate hospital in Richmond, one Laura Ratcliff. When she died in 1922, among her personal possessions were found many items belonging to Stuart, including a lengthy romantic poem which he had written to her. (Valentine Museum, Richmond)

Secretary of War Edwin Stanton, an unscrupulous man whose great ambition was to become president himself in 1868. He despised Lincoln and in private made fun of him with his Radical friends, calling him "the missing link." In an effort to establish himself as the most powerful man in America it is said that he intentionally prolonged the war by naming drunks and incompetents to positions of military leadership. Gen. George McClellan himself wrote Stanton a letter in which he accused him of intentionally undermining his efforts in the war.

According to Lafayette Baker, Stanton's chief of the National Detective Service, it was Stanton and Andrew Johnson who plotted Lincoln's murder. Following what many consider to be the unjustified execution of Mary Surratt, Stanton began telling friends, "That Surratt woman haunts my dreams." After his own death in 1868 it was widely rumored that he had committed suicide by cutting his throat with a straight razor. (Library of Congress)

On July 11, at Stanton's urging, Lincoln named Gen. Henry Halleck general in chief of all Union land forces. Petulant and erratic, Halleck was heartily disliked by all who knew him. His leadership was another in a long line of Union disasters. (Library of Congress)

Gen. Benjamin Butler, a political general and the power-mad "Beast of New Orleans" whom even Lincoln did not trust. He would later become a senator from Massachusetts and loudly accuse Andrew Johnson of being involved in Lincoln's assassination. (Library of Congress)

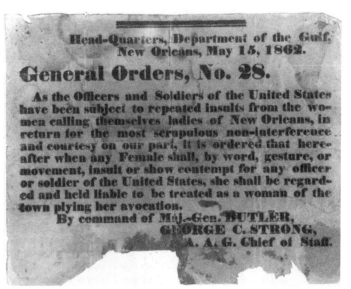

General Butler's infamous Order No. 28 informing the women of New Orleans that they would be treated as "a woman of the town" if they insulted Union soldiers. This order did nothing to endear Butler to people of the South, but it did make them fight with just that much more determination. (National Archives)

This anonymous Southern soldier, a member of the Hampton Legion, died early in the war during the Peninsula Campaign, the first large-scale Union offensive in the East. As can be seen in this photograph, he was able to apply a tourniquet to his leg but not to his shoulder wound and thus he bled to death, suggesting that he died alone. (Library of Congress)

Old friendships continued to run deep during the war, especially those friendships established by former students at West Point. Here, Col. George A. Custer, right, is pictured with his old West Point classmate and current prisoner of war, James Washington, member of a Confederate cavalry regiment and captured during the Peninsula Campaign. In later years Washington would write that Custer treated him more as a welcomed guest than as a prisoner of war. Custer's fame would later be enhanced by Sitting Bull at the Little Big Horn River. (Library of Congress)

General McClellan's retreat was so rapid following the Seven Days Battles, a series of battles that marked the culmination of the Peninsula Campaign, that he abandoned some twenty-five hundred wounded Union soldiers to the Confederate army. These pictured Union wounded are in a field hospital at Savage's Station, Virginia. (Library of Congress)

On August 4, 1862, Lincoln was urged to accept two regiments of blacks from Indiana into the Union army. Lincoln replied that blacks could not be taken into the Union army except as laborers. Here contraband slaves bury the dead following the battle at Cold Harbor, Virginia. It was hardly what Frederick Douglass had in mind when he and other abolitionists argued that blacks should be allowed to take part in the fight for their freedom. (Library of Congress)

In August, Lincoln wrote his famous letter to Horace Greeley in which he states, "My paramount object in this struggle is to save the Union, and is not either to save or to destroy slavery. If I could save the Union without freeing any slave I would do it, and if I could save it by freeing all the slaves I would do it."

Horace Greeley became a newspaperman at the age of fifteen in 1826. Later, in 1841, he founded the *New York Tribune,* which at that time had the largest circulation of any newspaper in the country. As its owner and editor, Greeley became one of the most influential journalists in the history of American journalism and a constant thorn in the side of Abraham Lincoln. Nevertheless, he recognized that Lincoln was a good man who had the misfortune to be surrounded and influenced by unscrupulous politicians, men who would stoop to any subterfuge, and those politicians hated the South.

Gen. John Pope, Lincoln's third Union army commander. In August of 1862 the Sioux Indians of Minnesota, who had been pushed off their hereditary lands, were literally starving to death. The Indian commissioner, when informed of their plight, laughed and replied, "Let them eat their own dung." Infuriated and hoping to reclaim their lands, the Sioux rose up and murdered some 350 white settlers. Pope's army went after them and very brutally subdued them. As a result of this uprising, 303 captured Sioux warriors were sentenced to death. Lincoln commuted the sentences of all but 39. This remains the largest mass execution in American history. (National Archives)

Here emaciated and ragged Sioux braves are sworn in at trial. (National Archives)

On August 5, Mary Todd Lincoln's favorite half-brother, Alexander Todd, pictured here, a colonel in the Confederate army, was killed at the Battle of Baton Rouge. Another half-brother, Gen. Samuel Todd, had been killed at Shiloh. A third half-brother, Dr. John Todd, served as a general and a physician in the Confederate army. (National Archives)

Another of Mary Todd Lincoln's half-brothers, Gen. George R. C. Todd served as a surgeon with Kershaw's Brigade from South Carolina. Early in the war he was accused of mistreating Union prisoners of war. Following the war he would spend the rest of his life practicing medicine in Barnwell, South Carolina. (National Archives)

Lincoln reading a draft of his Emancipation Proclamation to members of his cabinet on September 22. On the left are Edwin Stanton, seated, and Salmon P. Chase; William H. Seward is seated in front of the table; and from left to right, Gideon Wells, Caleb B. Smith, Montgomery Blair, and Edward Bates are behind it. It is obvious from this print that Lincoln had surrounded himself with rabid abolitionists. In time, it was inevitable that these men would influence his opinions and behavior. (Library of Congress)

Cartoonist Adalbert Volck of Baltimore illustrates a satanic Lincoln, surrounded by demons and with one foot on the Constitution, writing the Emancipation Proclamation. (The Lincoln Museum, Fort Wayne)

At the same time that Lincoln was drafting his Emancipation Proclamation, he met with Frederick Douglass and a contingent of blacks at the White House. Lincoln informed them that they were the cause of the war and that whites and blacks could never live together in peace. Douglass later responded that "the continued existence of slavery brands your republicanism as a sham, your humanity as a base pretense, your Christianity as a lie." (Library of Congress)

The Battle of Antietam in Maryland, September 17, 1862, became the bloodiest single day of the war for both sides. The Union lost twenty-five thousand men, killed and wounded, while General Lee lost a fourth of his army and was forced to withdraw to Virginia. This young Southerner gave his life for the right to pursue his own destiny. (Library of Congress)

Washington City. D.C.

Oct. 24.   1862

Maj. Genl. McClellan

I have just read your despatch about sore tongued and fatigued horses — Will you pardon me for asking what the horses of your army have done since the battle of Antietam that fatigue anything?

A. Lincoln

Following the Battle of Antietam, Lincoln wrote George McClellan that he should not have allowed Lee's army to escape. Angry over that letter, McClellan replied that his horses were too exhausted to go in pursuit. Lincoln then wrote the above letter in which he sarcastically asks what McClellan's horses have done since Antietam that has so exhausted them. (National Archives)

Lincoln on a three-day visit to Gen. George B. McClellan's headquarters near Antietam, Maryland, on October 3, 1862. After his visit, Lincoln reached the conclusion that McClellan "did not want to hurt the enemy." (Library of Congress)

Lincoln's appointment of Gen. Ambrose E. Burnside to replace McClellan as commander of the Army of the Potomac on November 7, 1862, has been called Lincoln's greatest mistake. When informed that Lincoln had selected him to replace McClellan, Burnside sputtered, "But I'm not fit to command an entire army." Lincoln should have listened. Little more than a month later, Burnside suffered a disastrous defeat at Fredericksburg, with losses in excess of ten thousand men. (National Archives)

These dusty Confederate veterans are on their way to Fredericksburg, where they would defeat an army twice their size. They have been called the finest infantry the world has ever seen. (Frederick Historical Society, Maryland)

The sunken road at Fredericksburg. Here Burnside ordered charge after charge against the entrenched Confederate positions, costing him thousands of casualties. These Southern boys died where they had stood only hours earlier. (Library of Congress)

Gen. William S. Rosecrans, who replaced Gen. Don Carlos Buell as commander of the Army of the Cumberland in Tennessee. He met Gen. Braxton Bragg's Confederate army on December 29 at Murfreesboro. Rosecrans' army outnumbered Bragg's army forty-five thousand to thirty-eight thousand, but the indecisive Bragg somehow managed to fight Rosecrans' army to a standstill. This is remembered as one of Bragg's better performances. (National Archives)

1863

Gen. Joseph Hooker, Ambrose Burnside's most vocal critic, was given command of the Army of the Potomac in January of 1863. In May of that year he met General Lee's badly outnumbered Confederates at Chancellorsville. Not only did he lose the battle, but his army was almost annihilated.

Hooker was a heavy drinker, and his army soon followed its commander's lax lead. The army developed such a following of prostitutes that these ladies became universally known as "hookers." A captain on his headquarters staff wrote Lincoln that "no respectable lady would dare visit Hooker's headquarters." (National Archives)

Reaction to Lincoln's Emancipation Proclamation, which took effect in January of 1863, was swift and harsh. In this very cynical cartoon by Baltimore artist Adalbert John Volck, a German by birth, the Republican Party is shown worshiping at the shrine of the American Negro. At the right of the Chicago Platform is the head of Abraham Lincoln. At the left is Henry Ward Beecher with a sacrificial knife. Charles Sumner bears a torch. Below is Horace Greeley carrying a censer. In the middle foreground is Benjamin Butler. Gathered around the Lincoln bust are Stanton, Seward, and other members of the cabinet. The statue is of John Brown, while Harriet Beecher Stowe is kneeling on a copy of *Uncle Tom's Cabin.* This might very well be the most damning political cartoon of Lincoln and the Republican Party to come out during the entire war.

One Southern journalist called Lincoln's proclamation "a fiendish triumph of fanaticism." Lincoln called it "the one thing that will make people remember I ever lived." In fact, this proclamation amounted to nothing: in reality it freed no slaves. But it did achieve its real purpose, to keep England and France out of the war on the side of the Confederacy. (Museum of Fine Arts, Boston)

Despite outnumbering the Confederate army 3 to 1, Lincoln's Union army was experiencing terrible problems in the Eastern theater, probably because it was pitted against two of the world's greatest military geniuses, Robert E. Lee and Stonewall Jackson. In the above print, *The Last Meeting,* Lee and Jackson are depicted at Chancellorsville in May of 1863. That night Jackson would receive the wound that would lead to his death a week later. The South never recovered from the loss of his leadership. (Museum of the Confederacy, Richmond)

White citizens in New York riot over the draft. These mobs were composed largely of newly arrived immigrants from Ireland and Germany who suspected that they would be among the first to be drafted. The riots began on July 13 and lasted for four days before Federal troops put an end to the violence. Over a thousand citizens were killed. (Davis Collection, Museum of the City of New York)

Rioters lynched any black citizens they could find and burned down a black orphanage. (Davis Collection, Museum of the City of New York)

The Federal government offered young men, Irish immigrants in particular, an opportunity to avoid the draft by volunteering for the army. Should they do so, they would receive a bonus of $402 for veterans or $302 for new volunteers. Draftees received no enlistment bonus. This particular poster seeks volunteers for the Irish Brigade, Twenty-third Illinois Volunteers. Desertion was always a huge problem for the Union army, especially following the Emancipation Proclamation. By war's end the army reported a total of 196,255 deserters, which was more men than General Lee had in his entire army. (National Archives)

This Irish immigrant to New York, a man obviously down on his luck, ponders the possibility of a most profitable military career, as promised on this recruiting poster. Thousands like him, men who had no desire to fight and die for the were thus lured by hunger into the army. (New York Historical Society)

Although blacks had been able to enlist in state militias since the start of the war, they were not able to serve in the Federal army except as laborers. Official government policy changed after the Emancipation Proclamation took effect and by the middle of 1863, the Union was actively recruiting African Americans. Here black soldiers from the 107th U. S. Colored Infantry were used in the occupation of the Carolinas following the war. Their officers were white. (Library of Congress)

Gen. George Gordon Meade, who defeated Lee's army at Gettysburg, waged from July 1-3. The South suffered twenty thousand casualties in this three-day fight, while the Union suffered twenty-three thousand. Gettysburg marked not only the high tide of the Confederacy, but also the turning point of the war. From now on, Lee must play defense. Meade, like McClellan before him, failed to go in pursuit of the Confederates but was quite happy to retire with the huge victory he had just won. (National Archives)

Gen. James Longstreet commanded Lee's First Corps throughout the war. He tried unsuccessfully to persuade Lee to assume a defensive position on the third day of fighting at Gettysburg, a move that might have saved the Confederacy. Lee had too much confidence in his army and refused to listen. (Library of Congress)

Gen. Lewis Armistead, who led Pickett's Charge at Gettysburg. One of his dearest friends was Union general Winfield Scott Hancock. Armistead received permission from General Lee to meet with Hancock at Gettysburg, but Armistead was killed and Hancock badly wounded before that meeting could take place. As Armistead lay dying he removed his gold watch from his pocket and requested that it be delivered with his blessings to Hancock. (Library of Congress)

It was said that Gen. Winfield Scott Hancock, seated, fought bravely throughout the war without regard for his personal safety. He and Armistead had served on the Western frontier together prior to the war and remained the best of friends. He received terrible wounds at Gettysburg and was brokenhearted when told of Armistead's death. (Library of Congress)

As the heroic Armistead and his few remaining soldiers from Pickett's Charge reached the low wall at the top of Cemetery Ridge, Armistead put his hat on his sword and shouted, "Give 'em the cold steel, boys. Who'll follow me?" At that point he and his men mounted the wall. He himself was mortally wounded and his few men driven back.

As a freshman cadet at West Point, Armistead had been severely reprimanded for breaking a heavy dinner plate over the head of senior cadet, Richard Ewell, who had been ribbing Armistead about a young lady. (Museum of the Confederacy, Richmond)

Confederate dead laid out for burial in a mass grave following the Battle of
Gettysburg. (Library of Congress)

The gory horrors of war. This Confederate soldier lies where he fell during Pickett's charge at Gettysburg. A Union cannonball has ripped open his body and severed his left hand, which can be seen lying just below his musket. The trigger finger of his right hand is still extended. Who he was, who his loved ones were, no one will ever know. Confederate dead were buried in mass graves at Gettysburg. Following the war their remains were moved to Elmwood Cemetery in Richmond. (Library of Congress)

Mary Todd Lincoln's very handsome half-sister, Emilie Todd Helm, and her husband, Ben Hardin Helm, a general in the Confederate army who was killed at Chickamauga on September 19. Mary Lincoln had now lost two half-brothers and a brother-in-law to Yankee bullets, leading to rumors in Congress that Mary Todd herself was a secret Confederate agent.

When Emilie visited Mary Todd immediately following her husband's death, Lincoln nearly came to blows with Gen. Daniel Sickles for stating that such a woman should not be allowed in the White House. Lincoln rose to his full height and responded, "General, neither my wife nor I appreciate advice from anyone concerning our guests at the White House." He then ordered Sickles from his office. It was one of the few times Lincoln ever lost his temper. (National Archives)

Gen. Daniel Sickles, a New York political thug prior to the war. He murdered the son of Francis Scott Key in a jealous rage after he heard rumors that Key was secretly seeing his wife. His commission was threatened when his entire division was nearly destroyed at Gettysburg because of his poor leadership. (Library of Congress)

Lincoln in November of 1863, at about the time that he delivered his Gettysburg Address, a speech that lasted two and a half minutes. Lincoln wrote that immortal speech during his brief train trip to Gettysburg from Washington.

His address is truly poetic, but some of his comments therein are open to question. Many believe that it was not the Union boys who "died to make men free" but the Southern boys.

Lincoln believed his main purpose in appearing at Gettysburg was to introduce the keynote speaker, Harvard's Edward Everett. The men were present for the dedication of Gettysburg National Cemetery. (National Archives)

Edward Everett of Harvard University and a candidate for vice president in 1860 was called the most eloquent speaker in America. At the dedication of the National Cemetery at Gettysburg on November 19, he was the keynote speaker and spoke for over two hours. (National Archives)

$$\mathfrak{Executive\ Mansion.}$$

Washington 186

Four score and seven years ago our fathers brought forth, upon this continent, a new nation, conceived in liberty, and dedicated to the proposition that "all men are created equal"

Now we are engaged in a great civil war, testing whether that nation, or any nation so conceived, and so dedicated, can long endure. We are met on a great battle field of that war. We have come to dedicate a portion of it, as a final resting place for those who died here, that the nation might live. This we may, in all propriety do. But, in a larger sense, we can not dedicate—we can not consecrate—we can not hallow, this ground—The brave men, living and dead, who struggled here, have hallowed it, far above our poor power to add or detract. The world will little note, nor long remember what we say here; while it can never forget what they did here.

It is rather for us, the living, to stand here

Lincoln's handwritten copy of the Gettysburg Address, which some have called the greatest single speech in American history. (Library of Congress)

A parade preceded the speeches at Gettysburg. (National Archives)

After the parade, crowds gathered at the cemetery to hear celebrated speaker Edward Everett deliver the keynote address. (National Archives)

A somewhat fanciful print of Lincoln delivering his Gettysburg Address.
(*Library of Congress*)

By proclamation Lincoln declared the last Thursday in November to be a day of thanksgiving. The first official observance was held a week after the dedication of the National Cemetery at Gettysburg.

This painting was based on several family photographs. Left to right: Tad, Lincoln, Robert, and Mary Todd. It was said that Lincoln and Robert always felt very uneasy in each other's company. (National Archives)

Gen. George H. Thomas, the so-called Rock of Chickamauga, relieved Rosecrans as commander of the Army of the Cumberland. (Library of Congress)

Adalbert John Volck's *Tracks of the Union Army* portrays a scene all too familiar throughout the South. Here a Confederate soldier returns from the war to find his home destroyed and his wife raped and murdered. Even his dog has been killed. (Museum of Fine Arts, Boston)

1864

The English press was highly critical of Lincoln and his war throughout the conflict. This cartoon, which appeared in the February 1864 issue of London's *Fun Magazine*, shows Lincoln burning George Washington in effigy and mocking him with the caption, "I'll warm ye! Your old Constitution won't do for the U.S." The fire is being fed by Lincoln's unconstitutional decrees, which are destroying the principles of American liberty. *(Civil War Times Illustrated)*

Gen. Ulysses S. Grant, whose name was unfamiliar to most during the early days of the war, was promoted by Lincoln to lieutenant general in 1864 following a number of victories over Confederate forces. He became the American army's first officer to hold that rank since George Washington.

Mary Todd Lincoln despised him for his drinking, his strong odor of cigar smoke, his slouchy appearance, and the number of casualties his army suffered. He is remembered by many for his infamous Order #11 of December 2, 1862, which expelled all Jews from his area of occupation. "They are, along with other unprincipled traders," he wrote, "dealing in black market cotton with the South." Lincoln, fearing a backlash from wealthy Northern Jews, had him rescind his order. (Library of Congress)

On March 8, the evening before he would formally receive his promotion to lieutenant general, Ulysses S. Grant was the guest of honor at a White House reception. It was then that he and Lincoln met for the first time. (White House Historical Society)

Grant's wife, Julia Dent Grant. She was the first cousin of Grant's best friend, Gen. James Longstreet, who commanded Robert E. Lee's First Corps throughout the war. Longstreet served as best man when Julia wed Grant. In 1868, at his wife's urging, President Grant named Longstreet ambassador to Turkey, thereby solving Longstreet's postwar financial problems. (Library of Congress)

By 1864, General Lee and his Confederate army, a mere ghost of its former self, were fighting on nothing more than courage and determination against the biggest and best-equipped army in the world. (Library of Congress)

Andersonville, Georgia, where so many Union prisoners died of sickness, disease, and starvation. The open latrine in the foreground doubtlessly led to much illness. Upon Maj. Henry Wirtz's arrival as camp commander, he was appalled to find neither food nor medicine for the thirty-three thousand Union prisoners kept there and pleaded with the Federal government for an exchange of prisoners. But Edwin Stanton, secretary of war, firmly opposed such an exchange. In the end, over twelve thousand Union soldiers died at Andersonville and Captain Wirtz was hanged for war crimes. Despite the horrible situation in Southern prison camps, more Confederate soldiers died in Union camps than did Union soldiers in Confederate camps, even though the Union had more than enough food and medicine for its prisoners. (Library of Congress)

In 1862 these Confederate soldiers captured at Fort Donelson were brought to Camp Douglas, the notorious Confederate prisoner of war camp in Chicago built on land donated by Lincoln's old antagonist, Sen. Stephen Douglas. Of all the prisoners of war brought here during the war, it is estimated that nearly eight thousand died of disease, starvation, and mistreatment. Many were actually tortured to death by vengeful guards. The camp's commander sold the bodies of dead prisoners to undertakers who then sold them to medical schools. Other bodies were simply dumped in Lake Michigan. The commander sold their food and medical rations to Chicago retailers. Certainly few of the prisoners in the above photograph survived the war. (National Archives)

On July 30, 1864, occurred one of the Union army's greatest debacles, the Battle of the Crater. Here, in hopes of breaking Lee's lines at Petersburg, Col. Henry Pleasants, a mining engineer, proposed to General Burnside that a tunnel be dug under Lee's lines, filled with gunpowder, and exploded. In all the confusion, Union divisions would then charge the lines and capture a large portion of them. Burnside, hoping to restore his reputation after his defeat at Fredericksburg, approved Pleasants' suggestion.

A trench 500 feet long was dug beneath the Confederate trenches and filled with 8,000 pounds of gunpowder. At the appointed hour an incredible explosion blew a huge portion of the lines. Gen. James H. Ledlie's First Division led the charge (Ledlie himself was far behind the lines drunk at the time). But instead of attacking the Confederates, men of the First Division immediately climbed down into the huge crater and began looking for souvenirs. A second wave of Union troops followed. It was Gen. Edward Ferrero's division of Colored Troops. Instead of attacking the Confederates, they too scampered down into the huge crater, laughing and joking and looking for souvenirs. Unfortunately for these doomed soldiers, the Confederates under Gen. William Mahone had recovered and began a counterattack.

Over the next hour the crater became a slaughterhouse. Burnside himself described it as "shooting fish in a barrel." Some Union soldiers managed to escape back to their own lines, but 4,000 were killed or captured. What could have been a great Union victory, with the proper leadership, became one of the Union's greatest losses of the entire war.

President Lincoln was not happy when told of this latest disaster and immediately relieved Burnside of his command. (Library of Congress)

Gen. William T. Sherman, who supported slavery, committed various war crimes against the women and children of the South during his fall March to the Sea. In an attempt to bring the war to a faster conclusion, Sherman and Grant decided to cut off Atlanta, the supply center of the Southern war effort, and bring the war to the civilian population.

Prior to the war Sherman served as president of Louisiana State Seminary, now Louisiana State University. (National Archives)

MARCHING THROUGH GEORGIA
By Henry Clay Work

Bring the good ol' bugle boys! We'll sing another song,
Sing it with a spirit that will start the world along,
Sing it like we used to sing it fifty thousand strong,
While we were marching through Georgia.

Chorus:
Hurrah! Hurrah! We bring the Jubiliee.
Hurrah! Hurrah! The flag that makes you free,
So we sang the chorus from Atlanta to the sea,
While we were marching through Georgia.

How the darkies shouted when they heard the joyful sound,
How the turkeys gobbled which our commissary found,
How the sweet potatoes even started from the ground,
While we were marching through Georgia.

Chorus

Yes and there were Union men who wept with joyful tears,
When they saw the honored flag they had not seen for years;
Hardly could they be restrained from breaking forth in cheers,
While we were marching through Georgia.

Chorus

"Sherman's dashing Yankee boys will never make the coast!"
So the saucy rebels said and 'twas a handsome boast
Had they not forgot, alas! to reckon with the Host
While we were marching through Georgia.

Chorus

So we made a thoroughfare for freedom and her train,
Sixty miles of latitude, three hundred to the main;
Treason fled before us, for resistance was in vain
While we were marching through Georgia.

This patriotic Union ditty, celebrating General Sherman's triumphant march through Georgia to the Atlantic Ocean, soon became famous throughout the nation, especially in that state and South Carolina.

This engraving of Sherman's March to the Sea depicts the destruction and devastation wrought upon Southern civilians. (Library of Congress)

Andrew Johnson, Lincoln's running mate in the presidential election of 1864. Johnson had been a semiliterate tailor before becoming a senator from Tennessee. He was infamous throughout Washington for his heavy drinking and was one of the few men whom Lincoln despised and planned to replace him in his cabinet as soon as possible. Many, including Mary Todd Lincoln, strongly suspected that Johnson was deeply involved in Lincoln's murder. (Library of Congress)

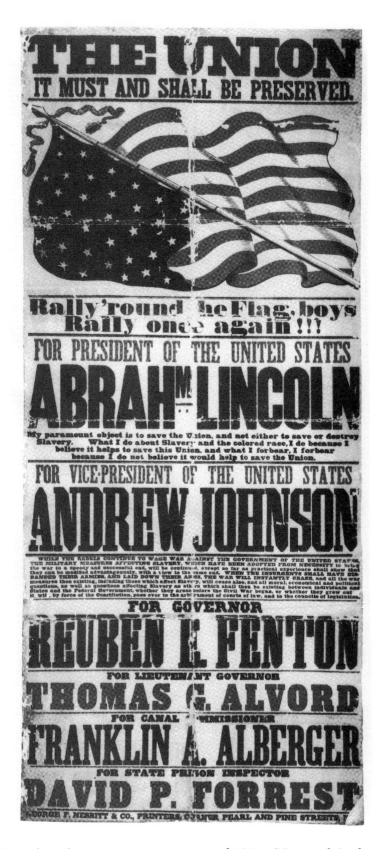

A Lincoln-Johnson campaign poster of 1864. (National Archives)

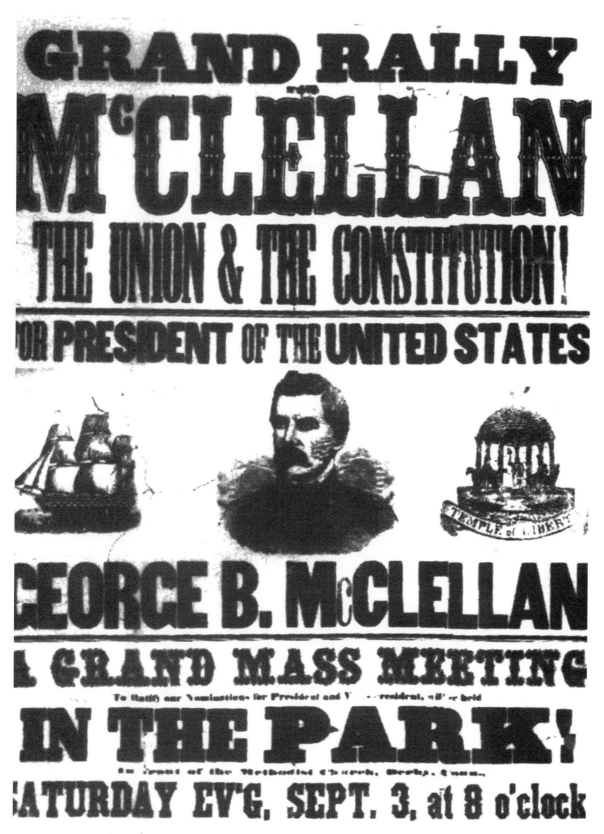

Lincoln defeated Democrat George B. McClellan by a large margin for the presidency in 1864, thanks to last-minute Union victories in Georgia and Tennessee. (National Archives)

1865

Lincoln and his son Tad, now twelve years of age. He and Lincoln loved one another dearly, played together constantly, and Tad would frequently burst in on Lincoln's cabinet meetings calling, "Papa day, Papa day," which was his way of saying "Papa dear, Papa dear." He would then fall asleep on a nearby couch. Following the meeting, Lincoln would very gently gather him up and place him in bed with him, where he slept almost every night. (Library of Congress)

Looking up Main Street from the State House in Columbia, South Carolina, on the morning of February 18, 1865. Sherman's Bummers had entered this undefended city the previous day. During a night of drunken debauchery, they hanged dozens of black slaves who could not tell them where their owners' treasures were hidden, and they burned Columbia to the ground. They attempted to burn a hospital where Union prisoners were being treated, but a dozen Union guards threatened to open fire if they did not leave. (Library of Congress)

Throughout the war Lincoln strongly denied that the Southern states could legally withdraw from the union and thus they were still part of the United States. With the war winding down in the spring of 1865, his denials cost him tremendous legal problems. If the Southern states had not legally withdrawn from the union in 1860-1861, as Lincoln had repeatedly stated, then they had the right, once the war was ended, to reclaim their place in the union and return the same politicians to Congress who had voted to secede. He had truly created an enigma for himself, one that he had not solved prior to his assassination. (Library of Congress)

Speaking from a temporary platform in front of the Capitol, Lincoln delivered his second inaugural address on March 4, 1865. It was during this speech that Lincoln made his famous statements: "With malice towards none; with charity for all . . . to do all that may achieve a cherished and lasting peace, among ourselves and with all others." These comments did nothing to endear Lincoln to the Radicals in Congress who dreamed of robbing and pillaging the South once the war ended.

John Wilkes Booth and his fellow conspirators can be seen in this photo. Booth, wearing a stovepipe hat, is standing on the porch above the president (just to the right of the statue), while Lewis Thornton Powell is standing below the president wearing a Western hat. David Herald is standing next to Powell wearing a dark cap. Booth later wrote in his diary that had he ever entertained the least intention of killing the president, he could have easily done so that day. (Library of Congress)

A closeup of the photograph of Lincoln's 1865 inauguration. Booth is standing on the balcony just above the president. Lewis Powell is standing below the president, wearing the Western hat. (Library of Congress)

Andrew Johnson, Lincoln's vice-president. He arrived quite intoxicated at the inauguration and insisted on making a rambling, drunken speech. Lincoln was humiliated and despised Johnson from thereon. He informed Sen. William Seward that he would dump Johnson at his first opportunity. Ben Butler would later proclaim that Johnson was behind Lincoln's execution. (Library of Congress)

Gen. Edward Otho Cresap Ord, his wife Malissa, and their daughter. In late March, hoping to escape the cares of Washington, Lincoln visited General Grant at his headquarters at City Point, taking with him Mary Todd and Tad. There, following an inspection ceremony led by Lincoln and Mrs. Ord, Grant and his generals treated the Lincolns to a fine banquet. During that banquet, Mary Todd stood up and shouted that Mrs. Ord was trying to steal her husband and demanded that Lincoln fire General Ord immediately. (She had previously accused Julia Dent Grant of the same transgression.) Following a stunned silence, Mary Todd fled to her room in tears. A humiliated Lincoln returned to Washington the next day. (National Archives)

In March of 1865, as the war wound to a dreary end, William Sherman, Ulysses Grant, and Admiral David Porter met with Lincoln aboard the *River Queen* to discuss plans for ending the fighting. Porter would later recall that Lincoln wanted peace on almost any terms. According to Grant, Lincoln stated, "Give them anything they want, if they will only stop fighting." As a result, Sherman and Grant were most liberal with their surrender terms for the Confederate forces surrendered to them under Lee and Johnston. (The White House Collection)

With the war coming to a close, this popular lithograph was published in newspapers throughout the North, depicting Lincoln, backed by Seward, Stanton, Grant, and other Union officers, extending the hand of friendship to Jefferson Davis and Robert E. Lee. The war was over and all was forgiven, Lincoln seems to say, nor would there be a harsh Reconstruction program for the defeated Southland. Instead, the South would be welcomed back into the union with open arms. (Library of Congress)

On April 9, 1865, his supply of manpower and arms long since exhausted and his last rail line cut, Gen. Robert E. Lee was finally forced to surrender the remnants of his once glorious Army of Northern Virginia to Gen. Ulysses S. Grant at Appomattox Court House. Following Lincoln's instructions, Grant made Lee very generous surrender terms, even feeding his army for the next week until they could begin their long treks home. (George Custer is standing at the far right in the above print.) (Museum of the Confederacy, Richmond)

Richmond, Virginia, in April of 1865, after the Union army had devastated the city. (Library of Congress)

Northern newspapers greatly exaggerated Lincoln's reception from the white population when he and Admiral David Porter visited Richmond at war's end. Smoke can still be seen rising from the destroyed city. Lincoln would be executed the following night. (National Archives)

This Confederate soldier was too young even to shave. He died in the trenches around Petersburg of a bayonet wound in the final days of the war. (Library of Congress)

This Confederate soldier was killed in a hastily dug trench at Petersburg by a shot to the forehead. Like most Confederate fatalities, who this boy might have been, where he might have called home, and who his loved ones were remains unknown. He is an Unknown Soldier, one of thousands. (Library of Congress)

The problems and worries of the past four years had aged Lincoln terribly. This image is believed to be from the last series of photos for which the president sat. Shortly afterward he would be assassinated by John Wilkes Booth while attending a play at Ford's Theatre. (Library of Congress)

Seventh: In general terms, — The war to cease: — a general amnesty so far as the Executive of the United States can command, on condition of the disbandment of the Confederate armies, the distribution of the arms, and the resumption of peaceful pursuits by the officers and men hitherto composing said armies.

— Not being fully empowered by our respective principals to fulfil these terms, we individually and officially pledge ourselves to promptly obtain the necessary authority and to carry out the above programme.

W. T. Sherman
Maj. Genl. Comdg
Army U.S. in N.C.

J. E. Johnston
General Comdg
C.S. Army in N.C.

On April 17, five days after Lincoln's assassination, Gen. William Sherman met with his old friend Gen. Joe Johnston at Bentonville, North Carolina, to accept his surrender. Recalling Lincoln's instructions from the month before, Sherman signed a liberal armistice granting sweeping civil and political concessions to the defeated South. Edwin Stanton, believing the South should be severely punished for its secession, flew into a rage when informed of Sherman's concessions and ordered him to again meet with Johnston and offer him a far more limited surrender agreement. Stanton, fearing that Sherman might run for the presidency in 1868, even went to the press and accused him of treason, hinting that Johnston had bribed Sherman with Confederate gold. A humiliated Sherman had no choice but to comply with Stanton's demand to renegotiate the terms. Joe Johnston, whose army had already departed to their various homes, had no choice but to sign.

In 1868, President Grant named Sherman commander of the U.S. Army. As such, Sherman dispatched his various armies to force the western Indian tribes to reservations all over the country—or to annihilate them. (Library of Congress)

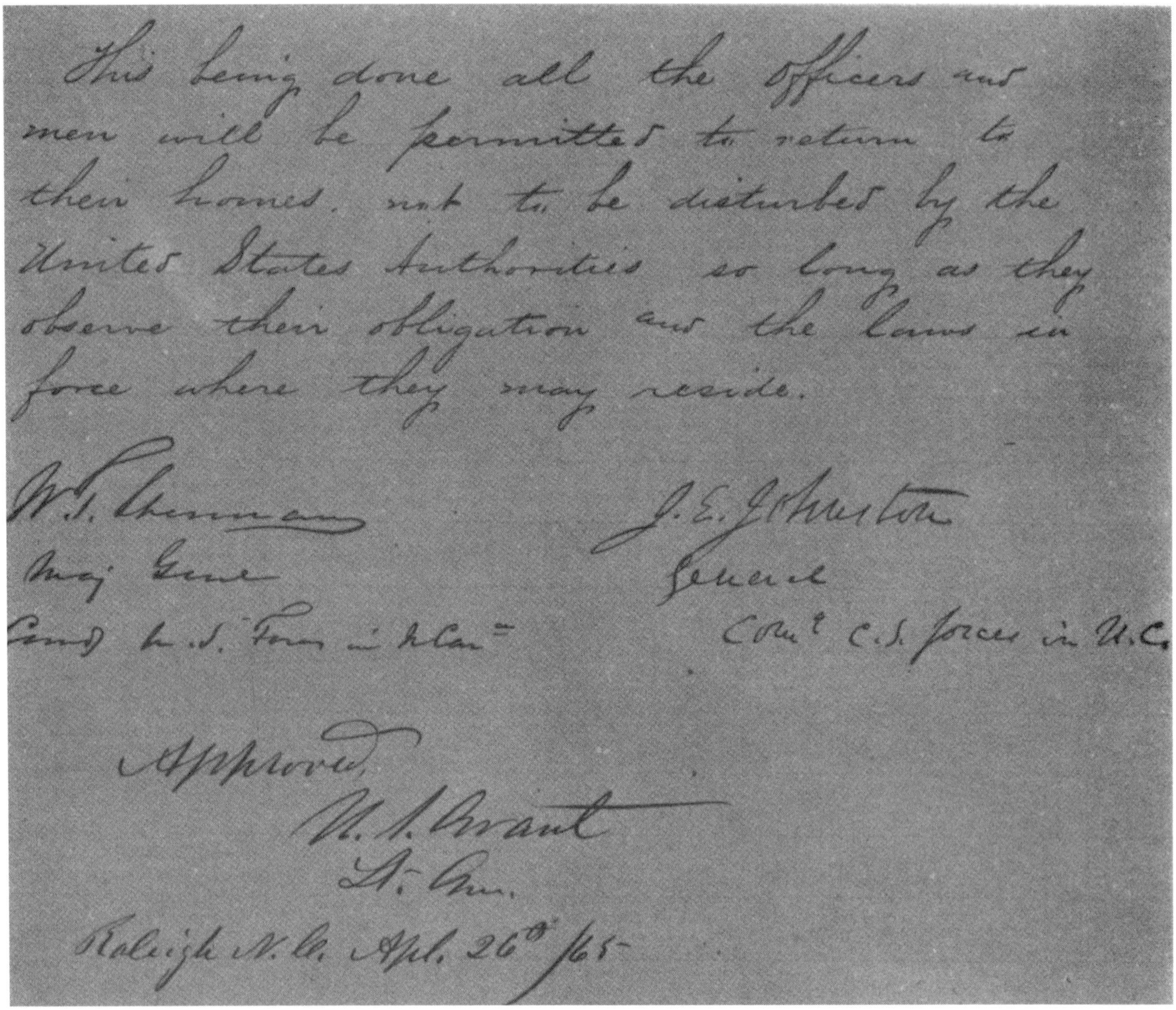

This being done all the officers and men will be permitted to return to their homes, not to be disturbed by the United States Authorities so long as they observe their obligation and the laws in force where they may reside.

W.T. Sherman
Maj Gene
Comd U.S. Forces in N.Car=

J.E. Johnston
General
Comd C.S. forces in N.C.

Approved,
U.S. Grant
Lt. Gen.
Raleigh N.C. Apl. 26th /65-

Sherman's far more modest agreement was signed on April 26. (Library of Congress)

The sinking of the *Sultana* on April 27, 1865, remains America's worst maritime disaster. Despite the fact that this boat was allowed to carry only 374 passengers, more than 2,000 expatriated Union POWs just released from Andersonville were crammed aboard to begin their long journey home. Cass Mason, the ship's captain, was paid five dollars per head. About 2 A.M., on the morning of April 27, the ship's boilers blew. Hundreds were killed in the initial blast, hundreds of others were caught in the flaming wreckage. It estimated that over 2,200 soldiers died in this tragedy. (Some 300 more lost their lives aboard the *Sultana* than died aboard the *Titanic*.) Yet, because of Lincoln's recent murder, news of the *Sultana* received little notice in national newspapers.

Some historians offer convincing proof that it was the Confederate Secret Service who destroyed the *Sultana*. The story goes that a Confederate agent, disguised as a sailor, slipped aboard carrying a twenty-pound hunk of gunpowder painted to look like a lump of coal. When that gunpowder was shoveled into the boiler the ship exploded. The Union army lost more men here than at the Battle of Shiloh. (Library of Congress)

On April 14, 1865, Maj. James Innes Randolph, a scion of one of Virginia's most illustrious families, stacked his musket and sheathed his sword for the last time. For him, as well as for thousands of other brave Southern lads, the war was over.

As Reconstruction got underway, Randolph sat down and composed a song that expressed the sentiments of most Southerners:

I'M A GOOD OL' REBEL
Major James Innes Randolph

Oh, I'm a good 'ol Rebel,
For four long years near about,
Got wounded in three places,
And starved at Point Lookout.
I cotch the roomatism
A camping in the snow,
But I killed a chance of Yankees—
And I'd like to kill some mo'.

Three hundred thousand Yankees
Is stiff in Southern dust;
We got three hundred thousand
Befo' they conquered us.
They died of Southern fever
And Southern steel and shot;
And I wish it was three millions
Instead of what we got.

I can't take up my musket
And fight 'em now no mo'.
But I ain't a-goin' to love 'em,
Now this is sartin sho';
And I don't want no pardon
For what I was and am,
And I won't be reconstructed,
And I don't care a damn.
Now that's just what I am,
For this "Fair land of freedom"
I do not care a damn.
I'm glad I fit against it—
I only wish we'd won;
And I don't want no pardon
For anything I've done.

I followed old Mars Robert
For four long years near about,

Got wounded in three places,
And starved at Point Lookout.
I cotch the roomatism
A camping in the snow,
But I killed a chance of Yankees—
And I'd like to kill some mo'.

Three hundred thousand Yankees
Is stiff in Southern dust;
We got three hundred thousand
Befo' they conquered us.
They died of Southern fever
And Southern steel and shot;
And I wish it was three millions
Instead of what we got.

I can't take up my musket
And fight 'em now no mo'.
But I ain't a-goin' to love 'em,
Now this is sartin sho';
And I don't want no pardon
For what I was and am,
And I won't be reconstructed,
And I don't care a damn.

Good Friday and
Its Evil Aftermath:
April 14, 1865

Ford's Theatre. On April 14, 1865, citizens in Washington were abuzz. According to the local newspapers, that night the Lincolns would be in attendance at Ford's Theatre and they would be accompanied by Gen. Ulysses S. Grant, the man who had just won the Civil War. Grant's military escort would be present.

At five o'clock that afternoon, Grant sent Lincoln a brief note: "My wife and I have decided to visit our children in New Jersey. Therefore I will be unable to attend the theater tonight." A West Point graduate, Grant was certainly aware that an officer does not snub a social invitation from his commander in chief. (In his biography, Grant would offer a brief explanation, saying that Secretary of War Edwin Stanton forbade him to attend.) Nevertheless, the Lincolns found new guests in Maj. Henry Rathbone and his fiancée.

At 10:15 P.M., the Lincolns were seated in the presidential box at Ford's Theatre watching the presentation of *Our American Cousin*. Without Grant's military escort, the only bodyguard for the president was John Parker, an officer from the Metropolitan Police Department, who was reportedly in a saloon next door drinking whiskey at that time. John Wilkes Booth entered the box and fired a single fatal shot from his Derringer at the back of Lincoln's head. (Library of Congress)

Maj. Henry Rathbone and his fiancée, Clara Harris, accompanied the Lincolns to the theater on the evening of April 14. Booth shot Lincoln then attacked Rathbone with a large knife, leaving him with a deep wound on his arm.

Years later, married to Clara and living in Germany, Rathbone stabbed his wife to death. He spent the rest of his life in a prison for the insane. (Library of Congress)

ASSASSINATION OF PRESIDENT A. LINCOLN.

This dramatic print show how John Wilkes Booth, with no guard to challenge him, walked into the president's box at Ford's Theatre and shot Lincoln in the back of the head, mortally wounding him. He himself would allegedly be murdered twelve days later in farmer Richard Garrett's barn in northern Virginia. However, there is some evidence that he made a clean get away. (Library of Congress)

The president's box at Ford's Theatre is on the right. After shooting Lincoln, Booth jumped to the stage, a distance of nearly twelve feet, breaking the small bone in his left leg. He shouted, "Death to tyrants" and made his escape. (Library of Congress)

This fanciful print shows the dying president surrounded by some twenty of his political friends, including Andrew Johnson, who had to be practically dragged to Lincoln's bedside. These people all saw Lincoln sometime during the night, but the room was far to small to accommodate them all at the same time. Lincoln died at 7:22 A.M. It was then that Edwin Stanton, pictured at the far right of the bed, removed his hat and made his famous statement, "Now he belongs to the ages." (Library of Congress)

On April 21, this special nine-car train carrying Lincoln's body left Washington for Springfield, Illinois. Here it is seen on a Lake Michigan pier in Chicago. (Library of Congress)

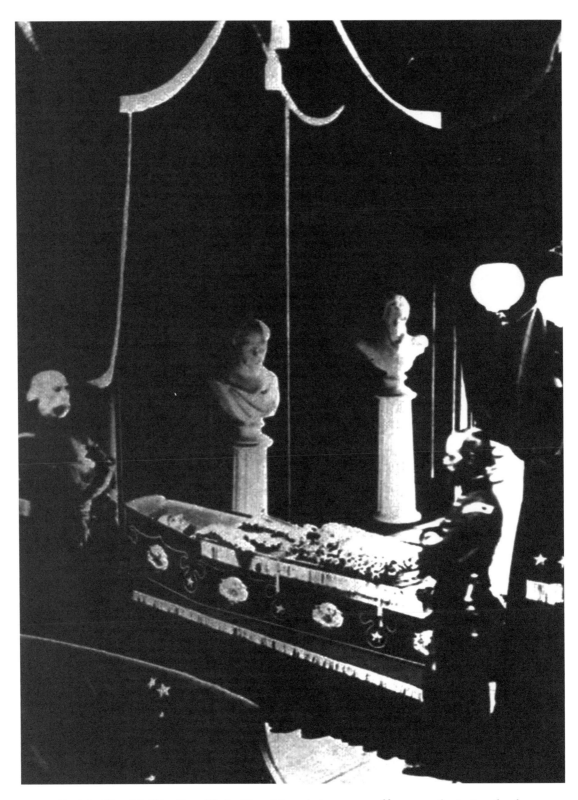

Inside City Hall in New York City, Lincoln's open coffin was photographed. Admiral Charles H. Davis stands at the head of the coffin, Gen. E. D. Townsend guards the foot. This is the only picture of Lincoln in death that was preserved. Edwin Stanton was furious when he saw this photo in the newspapers and severely reprimanded Townsend for allowing such a photo of Lincoln to be taken. (Library of Congress)

It was a dark and cloudy day when Lincoln's body arrived home in Springfield on May 3. Over the next two days his body would be viewed by thousands of mourners. His body was entombed at Oak Ridge Cemetery. (Illinois State Historical Society)

LINCOLN'S ELEGY
Walt Whitman

When lilacs last
in the dooryard bloom'd,
And the great star early droop'd
in the western sky in the night,
I mourn'd, and yet shall mourn
with ever-returning spring,
Ever-returning spring,
trinity sure to me you bring,
Lilac blooming perennial
and drooping star in the west,
And thought of him I love. . . .
With the tolling tolling bells'
perpetual clang,
Here, coffin that slowly passes,
I give you my sprig of lilac.

A reward poster offering $100,000 for the capture of Lincoln's murderers, even though the government at that time was unsure of their identity. Wanted for the murder were John Wilkes Booth; John Surratt, who according to later testimony was working for the Confederate Secret Service in upstate New York at the time of the assassination; and David Herold, whose name is misspelled on the poster. (Library of Congress)

John Wilkes Booth, who assassinated Abraham Lincoln, is thought to have acted in concert with high-ranking Federal officials. One of America's leading stage actors in the nineteenth century, he may have also been actively involved with the Confederate Secret Service in earlier efforts to abduct Lincoln and take him to Richmond, where he would be used as a hostage to force the Federal government to exchange prisoners of war. On March 20, 1865, Booth and recruited conspirators attempted such an abduction when Lincoln was scheduled to travel alone in his carriage to the Soldiers Home in Washington. Instead of Lincoln, however, it was Salmon Chase in the carriage.

On April 14, Booth's initial goal to abduct but not harm the president changed. Based on circumstantial evidence, it appears most likely that Lincoln was murdered because of his lenient Reconstruction program for the South, a program that the Radicals in Congress could not tolerate. The evidence further suggests that it was Edwin Stanton and Andrew Johnson who plotted that murder. Stanton then dispatched Col. Lafayette Baker and Maj. Thomas Eckert to visit Booth, a staunch supporter of the Confederacy, and convince him that the South could only be saved if he would execute Lincoln. (National Archives)

the whole, of the Austrian force engaged
of actual warfare, whereas the Danish army was co
young, middle-aged, and almost old, who had
fired in anger. That the Danes would have foug
doubts, but in war mere bravery is not sufficient
As it was, the troops suffered severely before the re
upon. The cold was intense; heavy falls of snow
followed by a partial thaw, which filled the air
vapour that soaked in their clothes and chilled
depressed their spirits to an extent which expe
enable a man to realise. Add to this that the
quately sheltered at night from the inclemency of
it will be evident to the most unexperienced perso
more hours would have rendered a considerable p
unable to fight from mere sickness. That Ge
wisely in abandoning the Dannewerk will even
even in Copenhagen, where the excitement was ve
its first becoming known. His determination
nearly every officer under his command comp
opinion, though there were some whose braver
their judgment, who gave way to expressions o
they heard of what had been decided upon.
Bishop Monrad that neither the Government
previously sanctioned the retreat; but it is im
cile this statement with the reports current in
King, when he visited the Dannewerk on the
agreed with Meza that the works were unten
small against an enemy so numerous. That the
the retreat is possible; but that General Mez

Col. Lafayette Baker, director of the National Detective Service, a forerunner of the Secret Service, worked directly under Edwin Stanton. In an 1864 copy of *Colburn's United Service Magazine,* he left a written record of Abraham Lincoln's murder that was not discovered until 1960, a record that has been called the most sensational discovery of the twentieth century. He writes that he left this message because he knew too much and feared for his own life, perhaps justly, for he was murdered in 1868, a crime that has never been solved. The day following Lincoln's assassination, he was promoted to general. (*The Civil War Times,* August 1961)

A page from *Colburn's United Service Magazine* for 1864. When subjected to an ultraviolet light, Lafayette Baker's signature became visible in the margins. (*The Civil War Times,* August 1961)

Maj. Thomas Eckert, director of the military telegraph and assistant secretary of war to Edwin Stanton. Lafayette Baker says the details of Lincoln's murder were left to Eckert. It seems possible that it was Eckert himself who first contacted Booth concerning Lincoln's murder. Baker and Eckert had both become aware of Booth's plot to abduct the president as early as February 1865, thanks to information supplied them by a Union officer who roomed in Mary Surratt's boardinghouse. Thus it was a simple matter for Eckert to contact Booth and arrange the president's murder. Indeed, at the moment that Booth pulled the trigger, Eckert's military telegraph suddenly went dead, and it was another six hours before the world learned of Lincoln's assassination, which gave Booth plenty of time to escape. The day following Lincoln's death, Eckert was promoted to general. (Library of Congress)

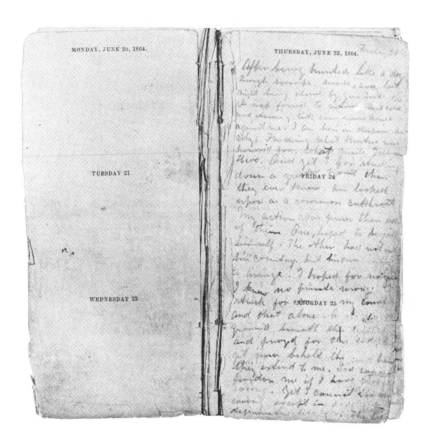

John Wilkes Booth's diary was found in Richard Garrett's barn. Lafayette Baker immediately turned it over to Edwin Stanton, who pocketed it and kept it a secret until 1867. At that time, during the impeachment trial of Andrew Johnson, the Speaker of the House ordered him to turn it over to the court. It then was discovered that someone had cut eighteen pages from the diary. Lafayette Baker took the stand and swore that the diary had been in perfect condition when he turned it over to Stanton. Stanton strongly denied it.

In the pages of his diary, Booth makes a most enigmatic statement. He writes: "I have a good mind to return to Washington and clear my name, which I feel I can do without any trouble." (Library of Congress)

Edwin Stanton, a henchman of the Radicals in Congress. He was an incredibly ambitious politician who dreamed of becoming president himself in 1868. In working to achieve that, he undermined Lincoln's positions and reputation at every opportunity. He was also infuriated by Lincoln's promise of amnesty for the South. (Library of Congress)

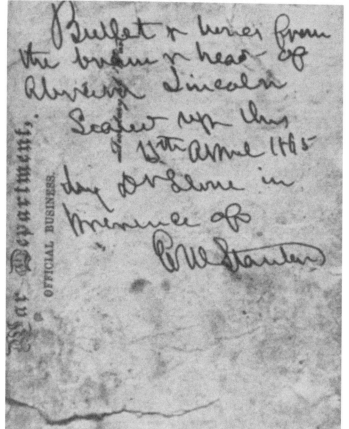

Edwin Stanton kept this envelope as a macabre keepsake. It held the bullet that killed Lincoln as well as numerous skull fragments. (Library of Congress)

In his designs for the presidency, Stanton reckoned without the ambitions of Andrew Johnson, who also dreamed of being elected president in 1868. Many accused Lincoln's vice president of intentionally prolonging the war in order to establish himself as the most powerful man in America. It was rumored that he committed suicide after Pres. Ulysses S. Grant refused to name him to the Supreme Court.

In a letter to her friend Sally Orne, dated March 15, 1866, Mary Todd Lincoln expressed the opinion of many when she stated, "That miserable inebriate Johnson had cognizance of my husband's death. Why was that card of Booth's found in his box? Some acquaintance certainly existed. I have been deeply impressed with the thought that he had an understanding with the conspirators & they knew their man. As sure as you and I live, Johnson had some hand in all this."

Johnson and Booth were indeed old friends, as Booth had acted on stage in Knoxville when Johnson was governor of Tennessee. There they had kept two sisters as mistresses and were frequently seen together in various Knoxville nightspots. (Library of Congress)

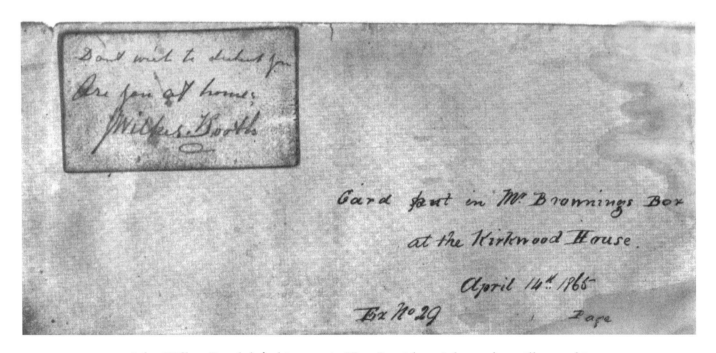

John Wilkes Booth left this note in Vice President Johnson's mailbox at his hotel, the Kirkwood House, on the afternoon of Lincoln's murder. Johnson swore that he had no idea why Booth would wish to visit him. (National Archives)

During the 1867 impeachment trial of Pres. Andrew Johnson, Benjamin "the Beast" Butler, now a senator from Massachusetts, rose to his feet and loudly accused Johnson of being a participant in Lincoln's execution. (Library of Congress)

From a legal standpoint, Booth's conspirators should have been tried in a civil court, but Edwin Stanton wanted to control every detail of the trial. He appointed a military tribunal, which was nothing more than a kangaroo court. Every one of the defense's objections was overruled, while every objection raised by the prosecution was sustained. It came as no surprise that all the conspirators were found guilty. Dr. Samuel Mudd, Samuel Arnold, Michael O'Laughlin, and Ed Spangler were sentenced to life in prison. George Atzerodt, David Herold, Lewis Powell, and Mary Surratt, the four persons known to have spoken to Booth on April 14, were all hanged. (Library of Congress)

John Surratt, whom Booth met in December of 1864. He was only twenty at that time, but he had nerves of steel and had already served as a trusted agent for the Confederate Secret Service for over two years, running dispatches between Richmond and Montreal. He participated in Booth's attempt to abduct the president but later swore that he was in New York on Confederate business at the time of the murder.

Two years after the murder it was discovered that he, a Catholic who had been studying for the priesthood when the war broke out, had been concealed in Montreal by several priests who had then arranged for him to book passage, under an alias, aboard a ship bound for Italy. There, he had remained hidden with the Papal Zouaves in Rome. After many delays on the part of the Vatican, he was extradited and at his trial in a civil court he was acquitted of playing any role in Lincoln's murder. Following his trial he would say only: "I traded my life for my silence."

He married the granddaughter of Francis Scott Key and became a prosperous Baltimore businessman. He lived until 1916. (National Archives)

Dr. Samuel Mudd, a country doctor, was convicted of aiding in Booth's escape early in the morning of April 15. Mudd pointed out that at 4 A.M. that morning, neither he nor anyone else was even aware that the president had been shot. A devout Catholic, he also swore three times under oath that the man whose leg he splinted on the morning of April 15 was not Booth. The man who came to him, he said, was six feet tall, had sandy red hair, and wore a false beard, which a number of witnesses later corroborated. Still, he was sentenced to life in prison. Andrew Johnson paroled him in 1867. (National Archives)

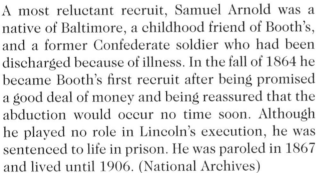

A most reluctant recruit, Samuel Arnold was a native of Baltimore, a childhood friend of Booth's, and a former Confederate soldier who had been discharged because of illness. In the fall of 1864 he became Booth's first recruit after being promised a good deal of money and being reassured that the abduction would occur no time soon. Although he played no role in Lincoln's execution, he was sentenced to life in prison. He was paroled in 1867 and lived until 1906. (National Archives)

Michael O'Laughlin was also from Baltimore and a childhood friend of Booth's. Like Arnold, he was not involved with the plot to assassinate the president, but he was sentenced to life in prison. He would die in prison of yellow fever in 1867. (National Archives)

Ed Spangler, a stagehand at Ford's Theatre, was accused of opening the rear door for Booth after he shot the president. For that little courtesy he was sentenced to life in prison. He was paroled in 1867 and, being homeless, was taken in by Dr. Samuel Mudd. (National Archives)

George Atzerodt, a native of Austria, operated a ferry across the Potomac River. Upon his arrest he revealed that Booth had assigned him to execute the vice president, Andrew Johnson, an act that the cowardly Atzerodt never planned to undertake. Atzerodt was hanged for his involvement. (National Archives)

David Herold was the son of a well-respected Washington family and held a degree in pharmacy from George Washington University. On the night of April 14 he met Booth in Maryland and remained with him until his capture in Garrett's barn on April 26. At that point he told the Union colonel in charge, "That man in the barn is not John Wilkes Booth." Herold was hanged. (National Archives)

Only nineteen years old at the time of Lincoln's execution, Lewis Thornton Powell was the most intriguing of all Booth's conspirators. A native of Live Oak, Florida, he was the son of a highly respected minister and the brother of a state judge. He was the most celebrated member of Mosby's Partisan Rangers before the Confederate Secret Service dispatched him to Baltimore to aid Booth in the capture of Lincoln. Once he met with Booth he operated under the alias Lewis Paine, and on July 7, 1865, he was hanged as Lewis Paine. The real Lewis Paine had been a friend of Powell's when he served in northern Virginia and would go on to serve as governor of the Montana Territory.

In 1998, 133 years following Powell's execution, anthropologists at the Smithsonian Institute discovered his skull among a collection of Native American skulls. How it came to be there, no one knows. It was returned to his family in Live Oak, Florida, for burial. (National Archives)

Mary Surratt, the widowed mother of John Surratt, ran a boardinghouse in Washington where Booth and the conspirators frequently met. She would become the first woman to be executed in America. Several years following her execution, the priest who heard her last confession wrote an article in a Catholic publication in which he swore that Mary Surratt was innocent of any wrongdoing. In later years Andrew Johnson wrote that Edwin Stanton forbade him to commute Mary Surratt's sentence as had been recommended by the military court. As for Stanton, during his last days in 1868 he told friends, "That Surratt woman haunts my dreams." Those friends said that Stanton did not die of natural causes but that he cut his throat with a straight razor.

It is suspected that Mary Surratt and John Wilkes Booth may have enjoyed more than a platonic relationship. Following her arrest a photograph of Booth, inscribed "To Mary," was found hidden behind another photograph on her mantle. (National Archives)

The boardinghouse of Mary Surratt in Washington where the conspirators frequently met. (Courtesy the Surrat House Museum)

On July 7, 1865, with the sun blazing down, the four condemned conspirators were led out to the gallows. They are left to right: Mary Surrat, Lewis Powell, David Herold, and George Atzerodt. (Library of Congress)

A grim photograph of Mary Surratt and Lewis Powell in death. Powell struggled for a full fifteen minutes before he finally strangled to death, a horrible way to die.

Earlier, while on the stand, he would not respond to any questions from the military commission. He refused to even give them his correct name so was executed under the alias Lewis Paine. He spoke only once and that was to swear to God that Mary Surratt was an innocent woman. (Library of Congress)

State of Tennessee—Franklin County,

To any Minister of the Gospel Having Care of Souls, Judges, or to any Justice of the Peace.

These are to authorize you, or either of you, to solemnize the rite of Matrimony between *Jno W Boothe* and *Louisa J Paine* of our County, agreeably to an Act of Assembly in such cases made and provided.

Provided, always, That the said *Louisa J Paine* be an actual resident in this County, otherwise these shall be null and void, and shall not be accounted any license or authority to you, or either of you, for the purposes aforesaid, more than though the same had never been granted, &c.

Witness, CLEM. ARLEDGE, Clerk of said Court, at office, the *24th* day of *Feby* 187*2*.

Clem. Arledge, Clerk.

It has been persistently rumored that John Wilkes Booth eluded government capture and was not killed in Garrett's barn as history records. The marriage license granted to John Wilkes Booth and Louisa Paine in February of 1872, in Sewanee, Tennessee, is possible evidence of this theory. According to Finis Bates, who wrote a book on Booth's escape, Booth lived in Sewanee under an alias for several months as a wealthy gentleman. He met Louisa Paine, a handsome widow, and they became engaged. On the day of their wedding he confessed to her his identity. She, a naive country girl, became upset and said that she would not marry anyone under an alias. Thus Booth was forced to sign his marriage license with his true name. Two years later he deserted Louisa and moved to Granbury, Texas. Educated citizens of Sewanee (the home of the University of the South) swear that the man living among them was indeed John Wilkes Booth. They did not report him, they said, because they had no love for Abraham Lincoln or the Union. (Franklin County, Tennessee, Archives)

In 1872, Finis Bates, an attorney, became friends with a prominent citizen of Granbury, Texas, named John St. Helen. In time St. Helen confessed to Bates that he was in reality John Wilkes Booth. He had managed to escape authorities in 1865 and had taken refuge with family members in New York and San Francisco. He knew all the details of Booth's life and had the scars and marks described on Booth. Here John St. Helen is pictured circa 1876. (The Swaim Collection, Georgetown University Library, Washington, D.C.)

Booth in 1864. In 1998 direct descendants of Booth, suspicious that the body in his grave was not that of their great-uncle, petitioned Green Mount Cemetery in Baltimore for permission to exhume the body for DNA testing. Green Mount refused, and a federal court later upheld their decision. (National Archives)

Living under the alias David George, St. Helen committed suicide in 1903. He had been dead for eleven days when this photograph was made at the funeral home in Enid, Oklahoma. Finis Bates, then a Memphis attorney who had once been St. Helen's best friend, visited the funeral home and stated that he recognized his old friend immediately. Bates claimed the body and shipped it to Chicago, where a team of doctors wrote that from the scars, broken bones, and other marks of identification, this body matched the description of John Wilkes Booth in every detail. Bates died soon thereafter and the body vanished; no one has seen it since. (The Swaim Collection, Georgetown University Library, Washington, D.C.)

Appendix

A Brief Look at Lincoln's Execution

Assassinate: 1: to murder by sudden or secret attack. 2: to injure or destroy unexpectedly and treacherously.

Execute: 1: to do what is required by a decree. 2: to put to death in compliance with a legal sentence.

By the summer of 1864 a great percentage of Southerners between the ages of eighteen and thirty-eight had been either killed or maimed on faraway battlefields while a like percentage had died of various illnesses in hospitals and prison camps. The South of course had no way to replace those men. Whereas Confederate forces had earlier found themselves outnumbered two to one, by the summer of 1864 those numbers were more like three and even four to one. Exacerbating the situation, by now the Union, with an unlimited supply of fresh troops, refused to exchange prisoners of war. The South warned that it had no food to feed Union prisoners nor medicine to care for their wounds and illnesses. But Edwin Stanton was adamant. There would be no exchange of prisoners. Union prisoners would be left to die of illness and starvation in Southern prisons.

It was then that several Confederate military leaders, in critical need of healthy troops, proposed a solution: they would abduct Pres. Abraham Lincoln, bring him to Richmond, and exchange him for Confederate prisoners of war. Desperate situations call for desperate measures, and the South by 1864 was truly desperate for manpower.

The South's desire to exchange prisoners of war was also motivated by humanitarian impulses. According to Federal War Department statistics, some twenty-four thousand Union soldiers died of wounds, starvation, and disease in Southern prisons during four years of war, a tragic statistic. Even more tragic, however, was that some twenty-six thousand Confederates died in Union prisons during that same period of time, this despite the fact that the Union army had a wealth of food and medicine it could have made available to Southern prisoners.

At Camp Douglas in Chicago, for example, it was later proven that the camp's commander had stolen food and medicine meant for the prisoners and sold it to retailers in the Chicago area at a huge profit to himself. He also sold the bodies of dead prisoners to undertakers who then sold them to various medical schools. Others he simply dumped in Lake Michigan. By war's end some seven thousand Confederate prisoners had died there of starvation and disease.

As for John Wilkes Booth, it seems that he had earlier become an agent of the Confederate Secret Service. He had been assigned to kidnap the president, not to harm him, and the best evidence suggests that the idea of assassination never entered Booth's mind prior to April 14, 1865, the day of Lincoln's murder. In fact, on several occasions Booth had been heard to remark that he felt a great deal of admiration for Lincoln the man. It was Lincoln the president whom he was sworn to abduct. But on April 14 something happened, something of such extraordinary magnitude that Booth became convinced that Lincoln must be executed immediately. What that something might have been is open to speculation, but Booth, by no means a stupid or violent man, was somehow persuaded that Lincoln must die.

There is evidence that it was not Booth who first thought of executing the president. Booth was merely a tool in the hands of high-ranking Federal officials who were yearning to rid the government of President Lincoln and Secretary of State William Seward, who advocated amnesty for the South now that the war was winding down.

Robert H. Fowler, an early owner and editor of *The Civil War Times,* devoted the entire August 1961 issue of the magazine (it would later become *The Civil War Times Illustrated*) to a startling discovery made by an unassuming New Jersey chemist, Dr. Ray Neff. Neff's hobby was studying the Civil War and collecting old books and magazines dealing with that episode. He had recently purchased an 1864 copy of *Colburn's United Service Magazine, Series II.* Reading through it, he discovered that someone had gone through the text with a pencil and made odd marks under certain words. Neff realized that someone had left behind a coded message. With the help of professional cryptographers, he was able to decode the message. It had been written by Lafayette Baker, Edwin Stanton's chief of the National Detective Service, and it gave a detailed account of President Lincoln's murder. Much information had also been written in the margins with invisible ink that became visible when placed under an ultraviolet light. Baker wrote that he left this message because he feared for his own life. He knew too much, he said, and suspected that he too had been marked for death. Perhaps he was right, for Baker was murdered in 1868, a crime that has never been solved. Ray Neff consulted with Robert Fowler, an authority on Civil War history, who felt that this article represented one of the most sensational finds of the twentieth century. And thus came its publication in the August 1961 issue of the *Civil War Times.*

Few will be surprised to learn that, according to Lafayette Baker, the prime movers in this scheme to rid the land of Lincoln and Seward were the secretary of war, Edwin Stanton, and the vice president, Andrew Johnson, both of whom were incredibly ambitious and equally unscrupulous. Stanton's greatest ambition was to see himself become president in 1868. With Lincoln dead and Congress in recess until December, the way stood wide open for a military dictatorship (with Stanton of course as the supreme dictator), which Stanton would settle for until the November 1868 election. But Edwin Stanton had reckoned without the unbridled ambitions of his partner in crime, Andrew Johnson, who also dreamed of becoming president in 1868. Johnson, unfortunately for his ambitions, had made a drunken fool of himself at Lincoln's second inauguration on March 4, 1865, and since then the humiliated Lincoln had snubbed him at every opportunity. Johnson recognized that his political career was over if Lincoln lived. But if Lincoln were to die, Johnson would immediately realize his ambition and become president of the United States.

According to the *Civil War Times'* article, "The Secret Papers of Lafayette Baker," Stanton, Johnson, and the Radicals in Congress quickly came to despise Lincoln because of his lenient Reconstruction plans for the South, and they were in a fever to rid themselves of him. To achieve their ends, Stanton plotted Lincoln's murder, then appointed the chief of his National Detective Service, Col. Lafayette Baker, and the assistant secretary of war, Maj. Thomas Eckert, to recruit the people needed to carry out his conspiracy. These men were all motivated by greed and a lust for power. And certainly the conspirators had nothing to fear concerning punishment or retribution since they themselves would be in charge of any subsequent investigation. In fact, Stanton and Johnson were well aware that they could manipulate any investigative committee, which would naturally consist totally of Union officers.

Having already angered the Radicals in Congress with his plan to restore the rights of the Southern states once they had returned to the union, Lincoln further turned them against himself when he began backtracking in his plans for African Americans. Abolitionists had assumed that with war's end, the president would set about making first-class citizens of millions of freed slaves, granting them the same civil rights as those enjoyed by white citizens. But now Lincoln would only agree that those "who were extremely intelligent and had served in the Union army" would be given the vote. In late 1864, Lincoln had confided in William Seward, "I cannot visualize millions of freed black slaves walking the streets of America." And now that the war was drawing to a close, he began repeating what he had said earlier, that all those former slaves would be much happier if the government continued the massive resettlement program that was sending freed slaves to South America and Africa. Dozens of boatloads had already deposited several thousand former slaves in faraway places.

Lincoln truly sealed his fate in early April of 1865 when he met secretly in his office with Judge John Campbell, a Virginian and former member of the Supreme Court. During that meeting Lincoln assured Campbell that he would allow the Virginia General Assembly to convene within the coming week at the State House in Richmond to discuss matters of importance now that the war was coming to an end. Lincoln also promised that he would order Gen. Godfrey Weitzel, commander of Union forces in Richmond, to furnish military escorts for the individual legislators as they came and went on state business. Lincoln was careful to order Weitzel to keep this matter strictly secret.

According to Lafayette Baker, Stanton's chief of detectives, Weitzel wasted no time in informing his boss, Edwin Stanton, of Lincoln's orders. Stanton flew into a violent rage and very brazenly countermanded the president's orders and instructed Weitzel to forbid the Virginia legislators to meet. Baker writes, "Then for the first time I realized his mental disunity and his insane and fanatical hatred for the president. . . . He laughed in a most spine chilling manner and said, 'If he would know who rescinded his order we will let Lucifer tell him.'" Two days later, as Stanton predicted, Lincoln was dead. Few find Stanton's words to be mere coincidence.

And what of Lincoln's secretary of state, the rabid Radical William Seward? His attitude towards the South had also undergone an abrupt change. Now he was preaching the same sermon of forgiveness that Lincoln was advocating. In fact, he had just recently shouted to a stunned Congress that the Southern states should be welcomed back into the union with all their rights restored. The war was over. Forgive and forget.

In the eyes of Stanton and Johnson, Seward was just as much a traitor to the Republican Party as Abraham Lincoln. Both men pondered the situation. Then, in a flash of inspiration, perhaps it occurred to them that it would indeed be fortuitous if both traitors, Lincoln and Seward, should tragically perish on the same evening. Not only that, but it could be claimed by Stanton, who would be in charge of the investigation, that their killers were John Wilkes Booth and his merry men, the wild-eyed stooges of Jefferson Davis and the Confederate government. With that they would they rid themselves of Lincoln and Seward, but they would also hang Jeff Davis and his rebel cronies in the bargain, silence them forever before they could ask too many embarrassing questions concerning the Constitution and states' rights.

After pondering Stanton's solution to the problem, Johnson might possibly have asked in his drunken drawl, "So you are proposing that we assassinate the president of the United States?"

Not the most tolerant of men, Stanton would have shaken his head in exasperation. "No, I am not proposing that we *assassinate* the president of the United States, Mr. Johnson. I am proposing that we *execute* a traitor."

It was a wonderful idea, the perfect solution to a true dilemma. According to Lafayette Baker, Stanton eagerly brought in Radical congressmen, Northern industrialists, bankers, and military leaders to discuss his Reconstruction plans for pillaging the South. Of course, he would then explain solemnly, Lincoln and Seward would have to be terminated for those plans to be realized. With dollar signs floating before their eyes, those who listened to Stanton's whispered lectures reluctantly agreed. Lincoln and Seward would have to be executed. Besides, traitors generally are executed, are they not? As reprehensible as such a move might be to them personally, it was certainly the best thing for America.

Once that decision had been made, says Lafayette Baker, Stanton assigned him and the assistant secretary of war, Maj. Thomas Eckert, to arrange the details of the execution. It must happen as soon as possible, before Lincoln could do any more damage to the party, before he could further broadcast his policy of amnesty for the South. The most likely time, in fact, would be Friday, April 14. That night, the Lincolns, accompanied by Gen. Ulysses S. Grant, would be in attendance at Ford's Theatre. It would be a simple matter for an assassin or two to slip into the president's box and execute him. Then it would be up to the assassins to plan their own escape, though they would certainly receive all the help the War Department could furnish. The War Department wanted them to escape—or die, since dead men tell no tales.

This reasoning would explain Sgt. Boston Corbett's murder of John Wilkes Booth on the morning of April 26. (Murder charges against Corbett were later dropped upon orders from Edwin Stanton.) It would also explain why the four conspirators who spoke with Booth on April 14—Mary Surratt, Lewis Powell, David Herold, and George Atzerodt—the day of Lincoln's execution were arrested and held incommunicado until all four were hanged on July 7, silencing their tongues forever.

It is a fact that the War Department had the names of Booth and his fellow conspirators as early as February 20, thanks to an inquisitive boarder at Mrs. Surratt's boardinghouse. It would have been a simple matter for Major Eckert to contact Booth. If such a meeting did take place, then Eckert could easily have persuaded Booth that Lincoln intended a vindictive Reconstruction policy, one that would totally destroy what remained of the South. But should Lincoln be eliminated, then Andrew Johnson, a Southerner born and bred, would become president. Booth and Johnson were old friends since both had worked in Knoxville, Tennessee, several years earlier. There, they had kept two sisters as mistresses and were frequently seen together in various Knoxville nightspots. But to ensure such a happy future for the South, Abraham Lincoln, along with his major henchman, the other old South-hater, William Seward, would have to be dealt with.

Once Booth and his conspirators were recruited, any eventualities were addressed. It was well known that Lincoln despised Andrew Johnson and was eager to dump him at the first opportunity. Would there not be certain individuals, people of great authority even, who might suspect that the ambitious Johnson had played some role in the assassination? After all, if the assassins wished to disrupt the functioning of the government, why did they attack the president and the secretary of state, instead of the president and the vice president?

For those who might harbor suspicions toward the vice president when he suddenly became president of the United States, Booth, likely at Eckert's urging, assigned George Atzerodt, the most cowardly heart east of the Mississippi River, to assassinate Johnson. Of course neither Booth nor Thomas Eckert ever intended for Atzerodt to actually move against Johnson. John Wilkes Booth, an unusually intelligent and perceptive young man, assigned the passive Atzerodt because he knew that the vice president would live forever if he waited for the German to murder him. The entire ploy, however, would divert suspicion from Andrew Johnson.

If Booth had truly wished to throw the government into disarray by eliminating the heads of state, he would have assigned Johnson's murder to Lewis Thornton Powell and not George Atzerodt. Had "the Terrible Powell" been given the assignment, there would have been no failure. By Saturday morning Andrew Johnson would have been just as dead as Abraham Lincoln.

This scenario also explains why Booth instructed David Herold to plant the revolver and knife in Atzerodt's room at the Kirkwood House on the afternoon of April 14. Atzerodt was a most suspicious character, and once authorities searched his room, they would find the incriminating evidence. Booth, an astute judge of human nature, knew that Atzerodt would crumble immediately before his police interrogators, and at that point he would reveal that it was he who, against his will, had been assigned to murder the vice president.

Maj. Thomas Eckert might also have promised Booth help from

the War Department in making his escape. Eckert was head of the army's Telegraph Office, which had functioned perfectly twenty-four hours a day during four long years of warfare. On the evening of April 14, at the precise moment that Booth pulled the trigger, the telegraph suddenly went dead. News of the execution and Booth's identity could not be telegraphed across the country for another six hours, certainly enough time for Booth to have escaped to the coast of Virginia, where he apparently hoped to catch a ship bound for Matamoras, Mexico.

Eckert might also have told him that sentries posted at the Navy Yard Bridge would be instructed to allow him to pass, and Union cavalry would not be dispatched to search the route he would surely travel until he had long since passed that area. Indeed, Union cavalry was alerted in such far-off areas as Baltimore, New York, and Philadelphia, but not on the route that any sane Confederate agent would travel to Virginia.

Nor did Booth need fear the presence of bodyguards at the theater. Although General Grant had planned to accompany Lincoln to the theater that evening, such was not to be. At five o'clock that afternoon he sent Lincoln a note stating that he and Mrs. Grant had suddenly decided to visit their children in New Jersey. He did not tell Lincoln that Stanton had confronted him that afternoon and forbidden him to attend the theater, thus leaving the way open for the execution to take place.

Once Lincoln received this note, he went directly to the Telegraph Office and personally appealed to Maj. Thomas Eckert, of all people, to accompany him to the theater. Eckert begged off, stating that he had too much work to do. Subsequent testimony would prove that Eckert was lying. He arrived home at 5 P.M. and did nothing for the rest of the evening but await the startling news from Ford's Theatre.

And of course Booth knew before he ever arrived at the theater that Lincoln would be alone and unprotected. Otherwise, why would he have armed himself with nothing more lethal than a single-shot Derringer? He had in his possession several six-shot .44 Colt revolvers. Had he anticipated any resistance, he would have armed himself with a Colt.

Eckert might have concluded his persuasive talk with Booth by pointing out that now Booth had only to agree to pull the trigger. Would Booth refuse and allow a tyrant to remain in office, or would he perform a deed that would win him the everlasting gratitude from citizens throughout the nation, especially those in his beloved Southland?

Two years later, during Andrew Johnson's impeachment trial of 1867, the Speaker of the House learned that Booth's diary, which had been found in Richard Garrett's barn, had secretly been in the possession of Edwin Stanton for the past two years. The Speaker demanded that Stanton immediately turn that diary over. In perusing that diary, the Speaker noticed a strange thing: someone had cut eighteen pages from the diary. Edwin Stanton was called to the stand and swore that those eighteen pages had been missing when Lafayette Baker turned it over to him two years earlier. The Speaker, puzzled by this matter, then called Baker to the stand. Baker stated, "I swear to God that that diary was in perfect condition when I turned it over to Mr. Stanton two years ago." Suspicion naturally fell on Stanton.

In that diary Booth makes a perplexing statement: "I have a good mind to return to Washington and clear my name, which I can do with little trouble." The Speaker read on from the diary. At one point, Booth mentions numerous accomplices in the murder, though he does not furnish any names. The Speaker and the senators were puzzled. Who were those accomplices? At that point, Benjamin "the Beast" Butler, now a senator from Massachusetts, arose, pointed his finger at Andrew Johnson, and shouted: "His accomplices? Who were they? If we had only the advantage of all the testimony, Mr. Speaker, we might have been able to find out who, indeed, were these accomplices of Booth; to find out who it was that could profit by assassination who could not profit by capture and abduction, who it was expected would succeed to Lincoln if the knife made a vacancy." Butler did everything but name Pres. Andrew Johnson as the moving force behind Lincoln's execution, an opinion held by a great many congressmen.

At this late date, it seems unlikely that anyone will ever know for certain the identities of all Booth's accomplices. It is known for certain that Booth did execute the president on the night of April 14, 1865, and with Lincoln's death his great and benevolent plans for a constitutional Reconstruction program for the South died with him. The same people who were likely behind Lincoln's murder then ravaged the South, a crime that outraged Southern Americans still remember today.

Bibliography

Angle, Paul M., ed. *The Lincoln Reader.* New Brunswick, N.J.: Rutgers Univ. Press, 1947.

————. *The Living Lincoln.* New Brunswick, N.J., Rutgers Univ. Press, 1955.

————. *The Tragic Years.* 2 vols. New York: Simon & Schuster, 1960.

Baker, Jean H. *Mary Todd Lincoln: A Biography.* New York: W. W. Norton & Co., 1987.

Baringer, William E. *Lincoln's Rise to Power.* Boston: Little, Brown & Co., 1937.

————. *The Lineage of Lincoln.* Indianapolis: Bobbs-Merrill Co., 1929.

Basler, Roy P., et al., ed. *The Collected Works of Abraham Lincoln.* 8 vols. Springfield, Ill.: The Abraham Lincoln Association, 1953.

Bryan, George S. *The Great American Myth.* New York: Carrick and Evans, 1940.

Cantey, James H. *The Genesis of Lincoln.* Greensboro, N.C.: Schnappsburg Press, 1939.

Catton, Bruce. *The Civil War.* New York: American Heritage, 1960.

Clark, Champ. *The Assassination.* Alexandria, Va.: Time-Life Books, 1987.

Coggins, James C. *The Eugenics of President Abraham Lincoln.* Greensboro, N.C.: Schnappsburg Press, 1939.

Donald, David H. *Lincoln.* New York: Simon & Schuster, 1995.

Fehrenbacher, Don E., ed. *Abraham Lincoln: A Documentary Potrait Through His Speeches and Writings.* New York: 1964.

Freedman, Russell. *Lincoln: A Photobiography.* New York: Clarion Books, 1987.

Griffin, John C., *Abraham Lincoln's Execution.* Gretna, La.: Pelican Publishing Co., 2005.

————. *A Pictorial History of the Confederacy.* Jefferson, N.C.: McFarland Publishing Co., 2004.

Hamilton, Charles, and Lloyd Ostendorf. *Lincoln in Photographs: An Album of Every Known Pose.* Norman: University of Oklahoma Press, 1963.

Hay, John. *Lincoln and the Civil War in the Diaries and Letters of John Hay.* Comp. by Tyler Dennett. New York: Dodd, Mead and Co., 1939.

Herndon, William. *Life of Lincoln.* Greenwich, Conn.: Premier Civil War Classic, 1930.

Hertz, Emanuel. *The Hidden Lincoln.* New York: The Viking Press, 1938.

Houser, A. M. *Lincoln's Education.* New York: Bookman Associates, 1957.

Kimmel, Stanley. *The Mad Booths of Maryland.* New York: Dover Press, 1969.

Kincaid, Robert L. *Joshua Fry Speed: Lincoln's Most Intimate Friend.* Harrogate, Tenn.: The Filson Club, 1943.

Kunhardt, Philip B., *Lincoln: An Illustrated Biography.* New York: Alfred A. Knopf, 1992.

Livermore, Thomas L. *Numbers and Losses in the Civil War.* Bloomington: Indiana Univ. Press, 1957.

Lorant, Stefan. *Lincoln: His Life in Photographs.* New York: Duell, Sloan and Pearce, 1941.

Lord, Francis A. *They Fought for the Union.* Harrisburg: The Stackpole Company, 1960.

McClure, J. B., ed. *Abe Lincoln's Yarns and Stories.* New York: Western W. Wilson, 1901.

McPherson, James M. *Abraham Lincoln and the Second American Revolution.* New York: Oxford, 1990.

Mearns, David C., ed. *The Lincoln Papers.* 2 vols. Garden City, N.Y.: Doubleday & Co., 1948.

Meserve, Frederick H., and Carl Sandburg. *The Photographs of Abraham Lincoln.* New York: Harcourt, Brace and Company, 1944.

Neely, Mark E. *The Abraham Lincoln Encyclopedia.* New York: McGraw-Hill, Inc. 1982.

Nevens, Allen. *The Emergence of Lincoln.* New York: Charles Scribner's Sons, 1950.

Nicolay, John G. *A Short Life of Abraham Lincoln.* New York: The Century Co., 1904.

Oates, Stephen B. *Abraham Lincoln: The Man Behind the Myths.* New York: Harper and Row, 1984.

Pratt, Harry E. *The Personal Finances of Abraham Lincoln.* Springfield, Ill.: The Abraham Lincoln Association, 1943.

Quarles, Benjamin. *The Negro in the Civil War.* Boston: Little, Brown & Co., 1947.

Randall, James G. *Lincoln and the South.* Baton Rouge: Louisiana State Univesity Press, 1946.

Rankin, Henry B. *Intimate Character Sketches of Abraham Lincoln.* Philadelphia: Lippincott, 1924.

Sandburg, Carl. *Abraham Lincoln: The Prairie Years.* Vols. 1 and 2. New York: Harcourt, Brace & World, 1925.

Shaw, Albert. *Abraham Lincoln: His Path to the Presidency.* New York: The Review of Reviews Corp., 1929.

————. *Abraham Lincoln: The Year of His Election.* New York: The Review of Reviews Corp., 1929.

Sparks, Edwin E., ed. *The Lincoln-Douglas Debates.* Springfield, Ill.: Illinois State Historical Library, 1908.

Stampp, Kenneth M., *The North and the Secession Crisis, 1860-61.* Baton Rouge: Louisiana State University Press, 1950.

Swanberg, W. A. *First Blood.* New York: Charles Scribner's Sons, 1957.

Tarbell, Ida M. *Father Abraham.* New York: Moffat, Yard & Co., 1909.

————. *In the Footsteps of Lincoln.* New York: Harcourt, Brace & Co., 1929.

Tripp, C. A. *The Intimate World of Abraham Lincoln.* New York: Free Press, 2004.

VanDeusen, Glyndon G. *William Seward.* New York: Oxford Univ. Press, 1967.

Warren, Louis A. *Lincoln's Parentage and Childhood.* New York: The Century Co.,1926.

Williams, Harry T. *Lincoln and His Generals.* New York: Alfred A. Knopf, 1952.

Wolf, William J., *The Religion of Abraham Lincoln.* New York: Seabury, 1963.